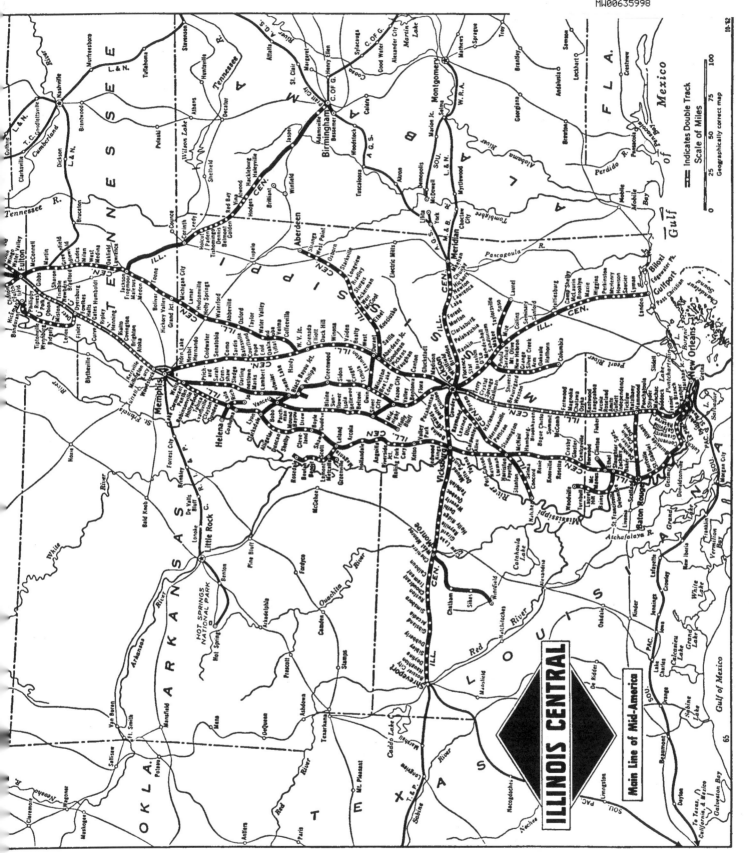

ILLINOIS CENTRAL

Main Line of Mid-America

ILLINOIS CENTRAL: SOUTH OF THE OHIO RIVER

WRITTEN BY KIRK REYNOLDS & DAVID P. OROSZI

FRONT COVER: The engineer on eastbound train ML-2 (Memphis-Louisville) opens up the throttle as the train pulls across the South Main Street crossing at Calvert City on November 11, 1980. The Paducah District was double track from Paducah to Gilbertsville Junction, about three miles east of where this photo was taken. (J. Allen Hicks)

BACK COVER: On a sunny October day in 1976, a southbound Illinois Central Gulf train emerges from Tunnel #2 at the prescribed speed limit of 25 miles per hour. The bore is the longest of three tunnels that were dug through the hills of the Shawnee National Forest. (Mike R. Schafer)

ABOVE: Northbound IC train #2, the "City of New Orleans," passes South Yard as it nears Central Station in Memphis on June 10, 1967. Behind the train is the small coach yard that serviced IC passenger equipment during its layover in the Bluff City. (William I. White, Steve H. Forrest collection)

White River Productions
PO Box 48
Bucklin, MO 64631
Toll Free: (877) 787-2467

www.WhiteRiverProductions.com

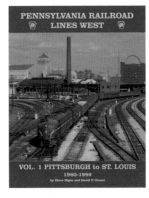

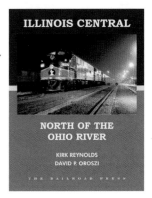

SOUTH OF THE OHIO RIVER

ACKNOWLEDGEMENTS

*T*his book completes a project that Dave Oroszi and I started in the late 1990s. We had initially envisioned an all-color book depicting the Illinois Central and Illinois Central Gulf from the end of steam until the merger with Canadian National in 1999. We had ambitiously planned to cover the entire railroad from Chicago and Council Bluffs to New Orleans and Birmingham in a single book of 136 pages.

As the text progressed and we gathered photographs, it became evident that we just couldn't properly show the entire railroad in a book of that size. To begin with, the history of the IC's northern lines was relatively straightforward while that of the railroad's southern lines was much more complex. We also found that, at the time, it was relatively easy to find quality color photos of the IC and ICG in Illinois, Iowa and Indiana, but color photos of the

railroad in its southern realm were more difficult to come by.

At that point, we decided to split our coverage of the Illinois Central into two books, divided by the Ohio River. The first, "Illinois Central North of the Ohio River", was published in 2003. With such an abundance of photos of the IC/ICG in Illinois, Indiana and Iowa for that book, we chose to cover the Edgewood Cutoff and the Eldorado District in the second book. Thus, these two lines in southern Illinois are included in this volume that showcases IC's system from the Ohio Valley to the Gulf of Mexico.

After the publication of the first book, we gradually found many more quality images of IC's southern empire as we met many of the contributors whose work appears here. Other contributors have also generously shared the work of other photographers from their collections.

As our photo selection steadily improved, work on the text moved forward and the book's structure took shape. We have tried to arrange the chapters in a manner that allows the reader to understand how each component of IC's southern domain evolved and was incorporated into the system.

Some of the reference sources used for this book include Carleton Corliss' centenary history "Main Line of Mid-America" and John Stover's "History of the Illinois Central Railroad." The IC's and ICG's employee magazine provided a month-by-month account of activity on the railroad, and information contained in the annual reports of the Illinois Central and IC Industries added another dimension to the railroad's history during its final decades.

Yet, there were many times during the preparation of this book when we sought information about a particular location, train schedule or date in history and, often, that information couldn't be found in a book, a magazine or in an employee timetable. That was when we turned to our "panel of experts" who usually had the answers to our numerous questions.

Fielding our many questions about IC's operations at Memphis were our four authorities on the railroads of the Bluff City: Steve Forrest, David Johnston, Phil Gosney and Mike Condren. Steve was an operator who worked at Missouri Pacific's Kentucky Street operator's office and has contributed several of the photos in this book. Dave also provided many of this book's photographs and answered many of our questions about Memphis railroads. Phil grew up watching IC's finest passenger trains making their station stop at Central Station and has also shared many of his photos for this book. Mike, who passed away in 2020, has hosted his wonderful "Memphis Railroad Pages" website for years, which has been a valuable resource that helped us understand this important rail hub.

For our coverage of the IC in Louisiana, we were most fortunate to be assisted by photographer and railroad historian Mike Palmieri. Not only has he provided a good portion of the photos featured in the sections covering the IC in the Pelican State, he has also shared with us his broad knowledge of rail operations in and around New Orleans.

We thank all of the following photographers for allowing us to share their work with you:

Photographers: Mike Abalos, R. D. Acton, Jr., Frank E. Ardrey, Jr., Richard Baldwin, David W. Beach, Jim Boyd, Charles F. Buccola, Charles B. Castner, Erik Coleman, Dennis E. Conniff, William C. Davis, Mark R. Demaline, Bill E. Dressler, Jerry Dziedzic, Steve H. Forrest, Curtis B. Fortenberry, Terry Foshee, Jack B. Fravert, Phil Gosney, Rick Grandish, J. Allen Hicks, Charles F. Hinrichs, James B. Holder, Raymond E. Idapence, James L. Jeffrey, David M. Johnston, Phillip Kotheimer, Charles Laird, Sr., R. M. Leach, S. A. Lee, David E. Lichtenberg, Scott D. Lindsey, James P. Marcus, Louis A. Marre, Mike McBride, Bob McCord, Morgan McIlwain, Lynn Moss, Randy B. Olson, Michael M. Palmieri, David Patch, Joseph R. Quinn, Jay J. Ruediger, Mike R. Schafer, Bob Schmidt, Alvin L. Schultze, Greg C. Sieren, Tom Sink, Jerry Sires, Tom Smart, Theo Sommerkamp, J. W. Swanberg, Tom C. Thornhill, William I. White, Mike Wild, Donald A. Woodworth, Jr.

In addition to the many photographers, we also would like thank the following people that opened up their collections to provide some of the images: Dan Dover, Paul Evans, Jack Ferry, Steve H. Forrest, John Fuller, Joe McMillan, N. J. Molo, and Cliff Scholes.

We also would like to thank Scott Withrow for creating the superb maps of Fulton, Memphis, Jackson and New Orleans. His dedication to detail and his patience allowed him to work through the numerous revisions of each map to ensure its accuracy.

Special thanks go to our proofreaders Jill Oroszi and Craig Sanders. Hopefully they caught all our mistakes.

Finally, we thank our editor, Jaime Serensits, for his enthusiastic support of this entire project, from the start of the first book through the completion of this one. It was his decision to expand the size of this volume to allow us to share even more of the photos that have been volunteered by our contributors. He has stuck with us for many years and we can't thank him enough for making the two books in this series possible.

ABOVE: The Illinois Central hosted two steam fantrips on the Kentucky Division in 1960, which were the grand finale of steam power on the IC. The first of these excursions was a Louisville-Paducah round trip that ran on May 14. The passengers were allowed to disembark to photograph IC 4-8-2 #2613 when it stopped at the Dawson Springs coaling tower to replenish its fuel supply. (Alvin L. Schultze)

INTRODUCTION

*T*he Illinois Central Railroad was a study in contrasts. Well known for its multiple-track main line south of Chicago and for its western main line across Iowa, the IC was also a railroad that served the Deep South. Among the factors that contributed to the IC's success was its direct route between Chicago and the Gulf of Mexico. After it was chartered by the State of Illinois, the line was built along the north-south axis of the Prairie State. These were the glory days of the steamboat on the Mississippi River and riverboats provided IC's passengers and shippers with connecting services at Dunleith (later East Dubuque) at the northwest corner of Illinois and at Cairo on the southern tip of the state.

At the beginning of the 19th century, New Orleans was the Gulf Coast's leading seaport. The city's commerce was closely linked to the river trade, but by the mid-1800s a number of railroads were planned to be built between New Orleans and the Ohio River. On the eve of the Civil War, three railroads connected to form what would eventually become the IC's first Cairo-New Orleans main line.

After the war, IC's directors saw it in the railroad's best interests to assist in efforts to rebuild those lines running north from New Orleans toward Cairo. For 12 years following the end of the war, the IC became increasingly involved in the operations of these southern roads. The construction of an extension from Jackson, Tennessee, to East Cairo, Kentucky, was financed through the IC. The IC took control of the route between East Cairo and New Orleans in 1877.

The opening of the IC's bridge across the Ohio River at Cairo in 1889 completed the railroad's Chicago-New Orleans main line. Over the next three decades, several new lines were added to the IC system on both sides of the Ohio River. By the mid-1920s, the IC was serving numerous southern cities such as Louisville, Memphis, Birmingham, Jackson, Mississippi and Shreveport, Louisiana. In western and central Mississippi, there were few places that were very far from the IC and its subsidiary Yazoo & Mississippi Valley.

This book is a tour of the southern half of the IC during the final decades of the 20th century. It covers the period from the early 1960s through the Illinois Central Gulf merger years to the Canadian National's 1999 acquisition of the IC. Our coverage will deal only with the lines that were part of the IC before the 1972 merger. We will begin with an overview of the history of predecessor lines south of the Ohio River.

North from New Orleans and Mobile

In the 1850s, railroad construction was flourishing across the states east of the Mississippi River. The Illinois Central Railroad was established to provide Illinois with reliable, all-weather transportation between the southern tip and the northern corners of the state. As the IC was being built, railroad promoters in Louisiana, Mississippi, Tennessee and Kentucky were also working to construct railroads that would reach from New Orleans to the Ohio River. Several lines were proposed, but only a few were actually built.

Of note were a group of three individual railroads that, together, extended northward from New Orleans through Jackson, Mississippi, to a connection with the Mobile & Ohio Railroad at Jackson, Tennessee. These lines were the New Orleans, Jackson & Great Northern Railroad, the Mississippi Central Railroad and the Mississippi Central & Tennessee Railroad. Promoters in Louisiana, Mississippi and Tennessee chartered these railroads in the early 1850s with the intention of connecting the Gulf Coast with the Ohio River.

At the time, building such a railroad was an ambitious undertaking. Much of the area that these lines would pass through was still wilderness, especially along the shore of Lake Pontchartrain north of New Orleans. After some false starts, these southern roads were completed in the late 1850s. The NOJ&GN/MC/MC&T route between New Orleans and Jackson, Tennessee, would form a direct rail connection through central Mississippi and western Tennessee.

The MC&T became part of the MC in 1859, just as the line from New Orleans to Jackson, Tennessee, was being completed. Traffic on the MC was handed over to the M&O at Jackson, allowing passengers and freight to connect with Mississippi River steamboats at Columbus, Kentucky. A 20-mile boat ride up the Mississippi and Ohio would reach the southern terminus of the IC at Cairo, Illinois. This was the first time that the traveling public had the option of a nearly all-rail route between Chicago and New Orleans.

The relationship between the M&O and the IC is rooted in the land-grant bill that led to the creation of the IC. In order to secure support for his bill that would provide land for the proposed Illinois Central, Senator Stephen A. Douglas enlisted the aid of his colleague from Alabama, William R. King. King supported a similar proposal for the construction of a railroad that would connect the port of Mobile, Alabama, with the Ohio River, enabling it to compete with New Orleans for this trade. An amendment to Douglas' legislation would set aside public land in Alabama and Mississippi for the proposed M&O. The land grant bill was passed by Congress and signed into law by President Millard Fillmore in September 1850.

The M&O main line between Mobile and Columbus, Kentucky, on the Mississippi River was completed on April 22, 1861. While the IC would evolve into one of the dominant railroads in the Midwest and the lower Mississippi Valley, the fortunes of the M&O paled in comparison. Most of the major military engagements of the Civil War took place in the southern states and the railroads of the region were often part of the battlefield. During the war, rolling stock, locomotives, track and facilities were commandeered (and sometimes destroyed) by both sides of the conflict. While the Illinois Central emerged from the war unscathed, the M&O struggled to recover and remained financially weak in the decades following the war. As fate would have it, M&O successor Gulf, Mobile & Ohio would eventually merge with the IC in 1972.

Illinois Central Looks South

During the post-Civil War years, the IC began looking beyond the borders of its home state. The railroad completed a bridge across the Mississippi River at Dubuque, Iowa, in December 1868, giving it a connection to the Dubuque & Sioux City Railroad, a line that IC now controlled. The D&SC reached westward from Dubuque across the state to Sioux City, Iowa, on the Missouri River.

At the other end of the IC, rail connections to New Orleans and Mobile lay beyond Cairo. IC president John M. Douglas sought to close the gap between Cairo and the M&O at Columbus, Kentucky. Given that the M&O didn't have the financial wherewithal to extend its own track between the two points, the IC looked for a better connection to the Gulf Coast.

In early 1872, former IC president William H. Osborn inspected the NOJ&GN and MC. Upon his return to IC's corporate offices in New York, Osborn recommended that the company's directors lend financial assistance to both lines. Both were controlled by northern financier Colonel Henry S. McComb.

In the spring of 1872, the IC entered into an agreement with the MC and the NOJ&GN. The IC underwrote the deal that secured financing for improvements to the two southern roads. Among the improvements was a 104-mile extension of the MC from Jackson, Tennessee, to East Cairo, Kentucky. The completion of the MC to East Cairo in December 1873 gave the IC a more direct route to New Orleans. The new car ferry "H. S. McComb" carried the first Chicago-New Orleans passenger train across the Ohio River on December 24, 1873.

ABOVE: Decapod #3619 was photographed working South Yard at Paducah, Kentucky, on this sunny afternoon in the mid-1950s. At the time, IC's conversion to diesels was well underway, but Paducah was one of the railroad's last bastions of steam. (Richard Baldwin)

McComb's NOJ&GN/MC route provided the IC access to southern markets, but the alliance was not without its problems. The Cairo extension was built to the MC's five-foot gauge, which was common for the railroads of the southern states. The difference in track gauges (IC was built to 4' 8 1/2" standard gauge) necessitated changing trucks on cars that were carried across the Ohio River at Cairo.

Of more immediate concern was the disparity in the condition of the two roads. The IC was clearly in better physical and financial condition. The company had earned its good standing by pursuing prudent operating and financial practices for the 20 years of its existence. On the other hand, Colonel McComb had only been involved with the southern lines since 1865 and the NOJ&GN/MC were still struggling to recover from the war.

In spite of the differences between the IC and McComb's lines, the arrangement apparently worked well enough for both parties. IC had its route to New Orleans, and McComb had a wealthy benefactor to bankroll his endeavors. During the first two years of the agreement, IC became a major bondholder of both lines.

In the wake of the Panic of 1873, the nation's economy fell into a depression, and traffic and revenues declined on both the IC and McComb's roads. In 1874, the Colonel merged his two lines to form the New Orleans, Jackson & Chicago Railroad. Two poor railroads became one poor railroad and IC's directors began to take notice of the impoverished state of its southern connection.

Even as a second transfer steamer was put in service at Cairo in 1875 to facilitate faster transit of equipment across the river, the financial condition of the NOJ&C continued to deteriorate. McComb solicited more support from the IC even though he already was behind on payment of interest on bonds held by the IC. IC president John M. Douglas and the railroad's directors realized that they were being exploited by McComb and would be forced to take control of its southern connection.

In late 1875, IC management initiated legal proceedings to place the MC and the NOJ&GN (courts did not recognize McComb's 1874 merger of the two lines) in receivership. They were successful, and receivers were appointed to oversee the reorganization of both lines in March 1876. Naturally, these men were sympathetic to the IC.

When the railroad properties, including their financial ledgers, were examined, both lines were found to be suffering from neglect and disrepair. It soon became apparent to IC management that they had allowed themselves to be taken advantage of by Col. McComb. To make matters worse, there wasn't much they could do about it. Any accusation against McComb would reflect badly on the IC and its representatives for their failure to catch any wrongdoing.

Henry McComb had acquired control of the NOJ&GN and MC during the economic and political chaos of Reconstruction, through means that would not have been possible during normal times. Unlike the men who conceived, built and ran the IC, and regarded it as an instrument for development, McComb saw railroading as a means to get rich quick.

As the MC and NOJ&GN cases moved through the courts, IC made preparations to purchase both lines when they were put up for auction. But Henry McComb still had a final card to play before the IC would be rid of him. In his possession were unpaid bond interest coupons from the two southern lines valued at $228,000. He offered to surrender the coupons to IC for $150,000 cash. With the payment he would also settle all claims and disputes between himself and the IC. In the interest of consummating the purchase of the MC and the NOJ&GN as quickly as possible, IC's directors decided to swallow their pride and pay off McComb.

The NOJ&GN was sold at auction to the IC on March 17, 1877. After several delays the MC was sold to the IC on August 23, 1877. The IC reorganized the NOJ&GN as the New Orleans, Jackson & Northern Railroad in May 1877 and the MC was reorganized as the

Central Mississippi Railroad in November that year. Both lines were merged on November 8, 1877, to create the Chicago, St. Louis & New Orleans. In 1882, the IC entered into a 400-year lease of the CStL&NO.

The rehabilitation of IC's new southern property was soon underway. The most demanding problem at hand was the difference in track gauges on opposite banks of the Ohio River. The remarkable task of converting 548 miles of the five-foot gauge East Cairo-New Orleans main line to standard gauge was achieved on Friday, July 29, 1881. Spikes for the new gauge were driven in advance and each section crew covered about a mile of track. The entire conversion was successfully completed in a single day.

The last major obstacle to be overcome on IC's Chicago-New Orleans main line was the Ohio River. Even with both car ferries operating at capacity between Cairo and East Cairo, traffic was backed up on both banks. Building a structure capable of spanning the Ohio River at its widest point without impeding navigation was still something of a challenge for the engineers of the late 1880s.

Design work on the new bridge began soon after approval was secured in the Kentucky legislature in March 1886. Construction started in the summer of 1887 and continued for two years. When the structure was put in service on October 29, 1889, the IC became one continuous railroad between Chicago and New Orleans.

Memphis, the Delta and the Gulf

While IC was busy acquiring its New Orleans main line and building its bridge across the Ohio, other interests were at work in

the vicinity. Collis P. Huntington, a veteran of the Central Pacific and Southern Pacific railroads in California, was making plans to build a new transcontinental railroad.

In 1869, Huntington's interests gained control of the Chesapeake & Ohio, a piedmont coal carrier. The C&O had run out of money while trying to reach the Ohio River and its promoters asked Huntington to step in and finance the completion of the road. Huntington intended to use the C&O as the eastern anchor of his projected cross-continent route. The C&O reached Louisville by way of a new line and trackage rights on another railroad in 1872.

Beyond Louisville, C. P. Huntington set up a new company, the Chesapeake, Ohio & Southwestern. The CO&SW acquired the properties of the Paducah & Elizabethtown and Paducah & Memphis Railroads in 1882. This would form the Louisville-Memphis segment of Huntington's transcontinental empire.

Memphis was becoming the commercial hub of southwestern Tennessee and was growing into one of the leading cities along the Mississippi River. On the other hand, the Delta region of northwestern Mississippi south of the city remained largely undeveloped. Huntington worked with Major Richard T. Wilson to build a new railroad between Memphis and New Orleans.

Construction of the Louisville, New Orleans & Texas Railroad was completed in September 1884 to connect Memphis with Huntington's Southern Pacific at New Orleans. With the completion of the Louisville-New Orleans route, Collis P. Huntington had his transcontinental system and the IC had a competitor in its southern market. The LNO&T opened northwestern Mississippi to the development of agriculture, which became the mainstay of the economy in the region.

ABOVE: In this view from one of Central Station's upper floors, train #3, the "Mid-American," arrives at Memphis on December 27, 1967. This schedule had been the Chicago-New Orleans "Louisiane," but its name was changed three weeks before this photo was taken. Along with the change of identity, it was truncated to a Chicago-Memphis run. The locomotives are passing the "Garden Track" where mail, baggage and passenger cars being added to or taken off trains were staged. On occasion, an office car would be parked on one of these tracks and the car's occupants would use the stairway to reach Calhoun Street. (Phil Gosney)

Realizing the potential for developing new traffic sources west of its own main line, IC sponsored the construction of its own subsidiary line northwest from Jackson, Mississippi, in the mid-1880s. The Yazoo & Mississippi Valley Railroad was completed from Jackson to Yazoo City in 1884. Within a few years, the Y&MV grew to become one of the IC's largest subsidiaries, operating a railroad that served most of western Mississippi.

Huntington's eastern empire was not financially strong and when it began to unravel in the late 1880s, IC saw the opportunity to strengthen its presence in Mississippi and reach Memphis. Bringing the Huntington properties between Louisville and New Orleans into the IC fold was accomplished under the leadership of two men: Stuyvesant Fish and E. H. Harriman.

Fish had first worked for the IC in 1871 as a clerk in the railroad's New York office before going into the financial industry during the middle years of the 1870s. When he returned to the IC, Fish was soon appointed secretary of the newly reorganized CStL&NO and was responsible for securing financing for IC's needy southern subsidiary. In the process, he met Edward H. Harriman.

Harriman was an accomplished stockbroker who had developed a reputation for reliability and integrity. He became involved with the IC in 1877 when he was given the position of secretary of the CStL&NO. He soon became a major stockholder of the IC and joined the board in 1883.

Stuyvesant Fish was installed as the IC's tenth president in May 1887 with E. H. Harriman being one of his closest allies on the board. Fish ran the railroad and Harriman managed the money. The Fish/Harriman administration embarked on a drive to improve the IC's physical plant. In addition, several new branches were added to the Illinois Central in Illinois, Iowa and south of the Ohio River. When it came to expanding IC's system, Harriman thought it made more sense to buy existing trackage than build new.

As the Huntington-Wilson interests were finishing the construction of the LNO&T in the summer of 1884, they made a threatening move toward the Illinois Central by obtaining control of the Mississippi & Tennessee Railroad. The M&T began operating between Memphis and a junction with the Mississippi Central at Grenada in 1857. While the M&T and MC were separate companies, they operated closely together; the M&T was built to the MC's five-foot broad gauge.

After the war, the M&T was acquired by Col. Henry S. McComb, who retained possession of the M&T after the IC took over the MC and NOJ&GN. Interchange between the two lines continued through the 1880s (the M&T was converted to standard gauge in 1881).

Following McComb's death in 1881, the M&T went on the auction block. In 1884, Richard T. Wilson took control of the line after submitting the winning bid. Wilson and Huntington soon canceled the M&T's traffic agreements with the IC, depriving it of a connection between Memphis and its main line. IC's president at the time, James C. Clarke, threatened to retaliate by building a parallel line to Memphis, but the feud was relatively short-lived. Huntington backed down and allowed E. H. Harriman to purchase control of the M&T in 1886. Harriman became the president of the Memphis line and IC signed a 400-year lease of the M&T in 1889.

By this time, Huntington's empire was beginning to falter. Though the LNO&T had grown to an 800-mile system that included several branches from its Memphis-New Orleans main line, it was not a strong railroad. Operating through a part of Mississippi that was still under development in the late 1880s, the LNO&T's revenues lagged. As bankruptcy loomed for the line, Collis Huntington decided to unload the property.

Fish and Harriman saw the LNO&T as a natural addition to the IC's southern lines and entered negotiations with Huntington to purchase the property. The LNO&T was sold to the IC on October 24, 1892, and was merged into IC subsidiary Y&MV.

During the following summer, IC was negotiating the purchase of another Huntington railroad, the Chesapeake, Ohio & Southwestern. The Louisville & Nashville was also involved in the CO&SW talks. It was initially proposed that the L&N take over the line and, in turn, grant trackage rights to the IC between Memphis and Fulton, Kentucky. But a dispute between the L&N and IC over the terms of CO&SW purchase erupted and the matter ended up in court, eventually going to the Supreme Court. The high court blocked the L&N from acquiring the CO&SW and IC finally took control of the line in 1896.

Acquisition of the M&T, LNO&T and CO&SW added over 1,300 route miles to IC's southern domain, giving it a route through Memphis. IC's southern main line shifted from Jackson, Tennessee, to Memphis. IC subsidiary Y&MV was the predominant railroad in western Mississippi and provided IC with a second main line between Memphis and New Orleans.

Rounding Out the South End

James T. Harahan succeeded Stuyvesant Fish in 1906 and served as IC's president for five years. Under Harahan's administration, IC established a route from Jackson, Tennessee to Birmingham, Alabama, using trackage rights over three other railroads and 80 miles of newly-built track. The production of iron and steel in and around Birmingham had made the city a significant source of traffic. Concurrently, E. H. Harriman had purchased a large interest in the Central of Georgia (with which it connected at Birmingham) to give the IC a friendly connection throughout the deep South and all the way to the Atlantic at Savannah.

Charles H. Markham held IC's presidency from 1911 to 1926 (with a 16-month hiatus during WWI, when he served on the United States Railroad Administration). During his tenure the last major additions to IC south of the Ohio River were made.

One of the greatest challenges he faced was to increase the volume of traffic that the Illinois Central was able to move across the Ohio River. The main line between Centralia and Fulton, Kentucky, was operating at capacity and the single-track bridge at Cairo was a choke point. Adding a second track to the bridge was considered, but deemed too expensive.

The solution to the traffic jam on the main line was to lay 168 miles of new track between Edgewood, Illinois, and Fulton. Engineering work for the new freight-only line, the Edgewood Cutoff, began in 1916. When completed in 1928, the new route gave the Illinois Central a second bridge across the Ohio River (at Metropolis, Illinois).

Numerous other improvement projects were carried out during Markham's term in office. Among them was the construction of a new passenger terminal and company office building at Memphis to handle surging traffic levels on the Chicago-New Orleans main line and the Yazoo & Mississippi Valley. On the Kentucky Division, a new line that paralleled the old CO&SW main between Dawson Springs and Central City was completed in 1924 to access new coal mines that were going into production. The following year, construction of a new locomotive backshop at Paducah, Kentucky, was started and opened in 1927.

The addition of two new southern routes in the 1920s turned out to be the IC's last major expansion in mileage. In 1925, IC purchased the Gulf & Ship Island, a line running from the state capital, Jackson, to Gulfport, Mississippi. The addition of the G&SI expanded IC's presence in southeastern Mississippi and gave the railroad access to another port on the Gulf of Mexico.

The following year, IC made an even larger addition to its system, as it added the "Vicksburg Route" in 1925. This was comprised of two railroads, the Vicksburg, Shreveport & Pacific and the Alabama & Vicksburg. The two roads met at Vicksburg.

The VS&P reached across Louisiana to Lorraine, on the Texas state line, although all of its through trains terminated at Shreveport, Louisiana. The Alabama & Vicksburg ran the opposite direction from Vicksburg to Meridian, Mississippi.

Poor Times and Wartime

As one of the most efficiently run companies in the industry, the IC was at its zenith when Lawrence A. Downs succeeded Charles Markham as president in 1926. The nation's economy thrived during the 1920s and IC prospered from growing freight traffic levels. Steel rolling stock replaced that of wood construction and bigger locomotives were built to handle heavier trains. The railroad's Chicago commuter operation was completely overhauled and converted to electric power.

All of these improvements were considered necessary by the company's directors (and World War II would prove them correct), but by the late 1920s, Illinois Central was heavily laden with debt. IC management determined that it could manage this debt as long as revenue levels remained strong. Unfortunately, events in the stock market in late October 1929 rearranged everyone's plans for several years to come. The market collapsed, and the nation's economy began an extended period of severe decline. The Great Depression had begun.

Over the next few years, IC's business dropped dramatically. The railroad posted an annual deficit of $3.5 million for both 1931 and 1932. During those difficult years in the early 1930s, IC struggled to reduce expenses to a bare minimum and still provide safe and reliable transportation. Employees were furloughed, pay scales were reduced and surplus equipment was put in storage. Bankruptcy loomed on IC's doorstep, but Lawrence Downs did not allow the road to slip into receivership.

Franklin D. Roosevelt was inaugurated as 32nd President of the United States on March 4, 1933, and, as part of his administration's "New Deal," the Reconstruction Finance Corporation was established to provide financial assistance to American businesses. IC received a loan from the RFC in 1932 to help it keep up with its debt. Although 1935 was the last year that IC posted a deficit, the final years of the decade were still lean ones. John L. Beven (better known to many as Jack) took IC's helm in December 1938, following Larry Downs' retirement.

While business conditions in America were slowly improving, the threat of war was brewing in far corners of the world. Japan invaded Manchuria in 1931 and moved against China in 1937. Italian forces invaded Ethiopia in 1935. A belligerent regime in Germany rearmed its military and provoked war with Britain and France when it attacked Poland in September 1939. France capitulated the following year, leaving Britain alone to stand against Adolf Hitler's Germany. While many Americans were reluctant to become involved in wars beyond the horizon, President Roosevelt realized the nation could ill afford to allow Britain to fall to fascism.

American industry began gearing up as the nation drew closer to the conflict. Carloadings of freight on the IC increased and more powerful motive power was needed. IC didn't have the resources to buy new freight power so a program of rebuilding steam locomotives was launched at the railroad's backshop at Paducah. The program produced a fleet of modern, reliable and capable freight engines that would carry the railroad through the next decade.

ABOVE: IC acquired a fleet of 125 2-10-2s in the early 1920s for heavy freight service. This wheel arrangement was called the Santa Fe type by other roads, but the IC dubbed its the Central type. Many of the Centrals, idled by the depression, were disassembled at Paducah and their boilers were used to create the new 2500-class 4-8-2s between 1937 and 1942. Wartime traffic put the remaining 2-10-2s back to work and all were rebuilt at Paducah during the war. One of the rebuilt Centrals, #2750, passes JK Junction as it departs the yard at Central City, Kentucky, with a westbound coal train in the fall of 1957. (Richard Baldwin)

ABOVE: Southbound train #1 is accelerating back to 79 mph at full throttle after passing a speed restriction just north of Covington, Tennessee. It's summer 1971 and Amtrak now operates the "City of New Orleans," but you would never know it by looking at the matching orange and brown equipment on this day's train. This train would soon get a variety of passenger cars from Amtrak's predecessor railroads still clad in their original liveries, providing a rainbow of multiple colors. Under Amtrak, this train's traditional all-day trek in daylight to the Gulf Coast was short lived, lasting only six months after the takeover. In November of that year, the trains would become #58/59 in a national renumbering scheme, renamed the "Panama Limited" and begin operating on an overnight schedule from both Chicago and New Orleans. (Phil Gosney)

By 1940, economic conditions were improving. IC and nine other railroads agreed to offer coordinated daily coach streamliner service between Chicago and Miami. There would be three trains, operating over three different routes between Chicago and Waycross, Georgia. All trains would run over the Atlantic Coast Line to Jacksonville, Florida. South of Jacksonville, the trains would run over the Florida East Coast to Miami. Each train would operate every third day.

For its contribution to the new service, IC placed orders for a seven-car trainset of lightweight streamlined cars along with a diesel passenger locomotive to pull it. The new streamliner was painted yellow and green and christened the "City of Miami." Once it left IC rails in Birmingham, it operated over the CofG, ACL and FEC.

At the same time, IC also ordered three "Motorailer" diesel self-propelled railcars and one trailer. In November 1940, one of the motorcars was assigned to the daily run between Jackson, Mississippi, and New Orleans under the name "Miss-Lou." The "Motorailers" didn't last long and were withdrawn from service by late 1942.

On the other hand, the new "City of Miami" was quite successful so IC ordered two more streamliners the following year. The new trains were to be built for IC's premier Chicago-New Orleans schedule, the "Panama Limited." Orders for four diesel passenger units and two dozen streamlined lightweight passenger cars were placed in early 1941. Work on the train was well under way when Japan attacked Pearl Harbor. When the War Production Board took over American manufacturing in early 1942, orders for new railroad equipment came under review. The WPB allowed the equipment for the "Panama" to be finished and delivered to IC. These new lightweight streamlined passenger cars were among last to be built for the next three years.

Jack Beven rallied the IC to the war effort as freight traffic skyrocketed and passenger trains filled with military personnel. Although civilian travel was discouraged during the war, the IC strived to continue to serve the needs of the public and industry.

As it turned out, the improvements that Charles Markham's administration undertook in the 1920s gave the railroad necessary capacity to handle the crush of war traffic. IC put both of its Ohio River bridges to full use during the conflict. The bridge at Metropolis was deemed so critical to the war effort that armed troops were assigned to guard it. As the primary seaport on the Gulf Coast, New Orleans was a key point of embarkation for troops, equipment and war supplies.

In response to increased traffic levels, the backshop at Paducah built 20 new dual-service 4-8-2 steam locomotives in 1943. These were the last new steam locomotives that IC would acquire.

As the final year of the war began, a change in leadership came to the IC. John L. Beven passed away suddenly on January 3, 1945, and IC's directors chose Wayne A. Johnston to succeed him. Having worked for the railroad since 1918, Johnston was a man of thrift and vigilance. Nonetheless, his administration would invest heavily to rebuild and modernize the IC through the 1950s.

Prosperity, then Reality

When the war ended, and restrictions were removed on the manufacture of railroad equipment, IC went on a shopping spree. New lightweight, streamlined and diesel-powered passenger trains were delivered and more diesel switchers were purchased for yard service. Track was rehabilitated and other structures were repaired. In the early 1950s, the Cairo Bridge was rebuilt with completely new spans. Nonconnah Yard on the south side of Memphis was rebuilt and had its name changed to Johnston Yard. A new joint passenger terminal at New Orleans was opened in 1954.

During this period, IC also pursued an aggressive program of debt reduction. The traffic surge during the war years had produced record revenues and this prosperity provided the cash to pay off financial obligations that had accumulated during the 1920s and 1930s. The company also trimmed its bureaucracy by merging its southern subsidiary lines into the IC proper.

In spite of these improvements, IC faced a difficult future. The regulatory process lagged a half-century behind the rail industry's latest technical improvements. Construction of highways allowed more automobiles and trucks to take traffic away from railroads. Air travel rendered even the newest streamliners too slow to be competitive. Passenger revenues fell while railroads were mandated to continue offering service that most of the traveling public didn't want.

Confronted with increasing competition, Wayne Johnston became one of the industry's most outspoken proponents for deregulation of the railroads. Eventually, he realized that in order to make an acceptable return on investment, IC had to become more than a railroad. A new holding company, Illinois Central Industries, was incorporated in August 1962 to allow IC to enter into non-rail enterprises such as real estate and manufacturing. During its first years, the new holding company made few acquisitions.

In 1966, Wayne Johnston was preparing to retire, and William B. Johnson was elected to take the helm of the railroad as well as Illinois Central Industries. Johnson had reorganized Railway Express Agency in the early 1960s and he brought to the IC a style of management that was quite different from Wayne Johnston's. The new president went to work on May 2, 1966, and began the transformation of the company into a diversified conglomerate. Valuable tracts of railroad-owned real estate were sold to raise money for the purchase of businesses outside of the rail industry.

IC and GM&O negotiated a merger agreement that was approved at the end of 1971. The merger was implemented in August 1972 and the "new" railroad was named Illinois Central Gulf. By the mid-1970s, IC Industries had established its presence in industrial and consumer markets and was making far better profits by selling soda pop than running a 9,600-mile railroad. The holding company decided to either merge its railroad with another or sell it in its entirety. Talks with Southern Railway took place in late 1978, but ended when the two parties could not resolve their differences.

A pivotal development was the passage of the Staggers Rail Act of 1980 that allowed the deregulation of the rail industry. This simplified the process that permitted railroads to sell or abandon unwanted trackage and made it easier for new companies to enter the railroad business. ICG began selling large parcels of trackage, along with locomotives and rolling stock, to spawn several new regional railroads.

The sale of three large pieces of former IC property south of the Ohio River in 1985-86 resulted in the creation of new regional railroads: Gulf & Mississippi, MidSouth Rail and Paducah & Louisville. The first large-scale sale was to G&M, which acquired a network of former GM&O lines concentrated in eastern Mississippi in 1985. The following year, MidSouth Rail bought ICG's Shreveport-Meridian route and the P&L took control of ICG's Kentucky Division from Paducah to Louisville.

Illinois Central Gulf also abandoned many miles track in the 1980s and by the end of the decade the railroad had been pruned down to a 3,000-mile core system. But IC Industries still couldn't find a buyer. Determined to leave the rail industry, the holding company decided to try a new approach.

The Final Decade

In September 1987, IC Industries announced that it would spin the ICG off by distributing common stock of the railroad to IC Industries shareholders. ICI changed its name to Whitman Corporation and dropped Gulf from the railroad's name. The "new" IC was spun off on December 31, 1988, under the name Illinois Central Transportation Company.

ABOVE: During the 16-year life of the Illinois Central Gulf, its fleet of diesels wore no less than eight different paint schemes. At the East Thomas Yard engine facility in Birmingham, an ICG engine consist sports three of those schemes in March 1975. (Curtis B. Fortenberry)

ABOVE: IC GP38-2 #9571 takes a northbound local over the long trestle that carries the McComb District across the Bonnet Carre Spillway at Frenier, Louisiana, in September 1999. This engine was built for the GM&O just before the merger in 1972. (David W. Beach)

Six weeks later, an investment firm offered to purchase all ICTC stock. The shareholders accepted and the new IC came under the control of the Prospect Group. Prospect Group had held controlling interest in MidSouth Rail before making its ICTC stock offer. Following acceptance of that bid, Prospect sold its stake in MidSouth to avoid a conflict of interest.

To head the new company, Prospect brought in the former president of MidSouth, Edward Moyers. When Whitman spun off the IC, Moyers saw an opportunity to transform the trimmed-down railroad into a profitable enterprise, so he convinced Prospect Group's management to make its offer. Moyers himself was an IC veteran, having begun his railroad career there.

Among the many changes that his administration implemented was the conversion of the Chicago-New Orleans main line to a single-track railroad that was dispatched by centralized traffic control. This resulted in the rebuilding of the former Y&MV between Memphis and Jackson, Mississippi, and the removal of the second main track north of Memphis and south of Jackson. The new CTC system operated new block signals (a first for that part of the Y&MV) and power switches on mainline sidings. Upon completion of the projects, traffic on IC's Chicago-New Orleans main line was controlled from a new dispatching center in the Chicago suburb of Homewood.

When Moyers retired in early 1993, E. Hunter Harrison took over. Continuing a strategy of maximum utilization of resources, Harrison reduced Illinois Central's operating ratio (the percentage of income spent on operating costs) to among the lowest in the industry. In 1996, IC acquired the holdings of Chicago Central & Pacific, a regional railroad that was created in 1985 from the sale of IC's Iowa main line. The IC once again reached westward across the states of Illinois and Iowa.

As the century drew to a close, North American railroads were consolidating into a handful of mega-systems. Union Pacific absorbed Chicago & North Western and then Southern Pacific.

Burlington Northern joined forces with Santa Fe. Norfolk Southern and CSX divided Conrail between themselves. Just where IC would fit into this mix was uncertain. IC engaged in negotiations with Kansas City Southern in 1994 and by mid-summer the two roads put forth a letter of intent to merge. The deal fell apart that autumn, but IC continued its search for a partner.

That partner turned out to be Canadian National Railway. CN purchased the IC in 1999 and made it a subsidiary. IC operations were integrated into the CN system while the IC corporate image was maintained through the railroad's sesquicentennial in 2001. After CN acquired Wisconsin Central Railroad in 2002, the company embarked on a "single identity" campaign. Henceforth, all business was to be conducted under the CN service mark. While the IC still survives as a "paper" railroad, new paint and new signs now identify the property as CN.

Though the CN does not operate in many of the locales that the IC once did, much of what remains of the IC is a vital part of a rail system that spans North America, encircles the Great Lakes and reaches to the Gulf of Mexico. Many other rail lines that had once been part of the IC (but were sold off by ICG and the latter-day IC) also continue to serve, either as part of a Class I system, a regional railroad or a short line. In a number of cities, towns and villages in Tennessee, Louisiana and Mississippi, the local IC depot or freight house has been renovated and houses a business, museum or community center.

In 2021, trains still rolled through places such as Crenshaw, Mississippi, Ponchitoula, Louisiana, and Leitchfield, Kentucky, every day. In towns like Tunica, Mississippi, Boliver, Tennessee, and Hackleburg, Alabama, the tracks have been gone for years. But in all of those places, the IC was more than just a railroad, made up of trains, tracks and buildings. It was an institution, built and run by people who took pride in their work. Their legacy is that institution that will always be known as the Main Line of Mid-America.

The Edgewood Cutoff – Shortcut through Egypt

Following the completion of Illinois Central's main line in 1856, traffic grew at a steady pace for the next 50 years. Then during the first decade of the 20th century, traffic volume on the Illinois Central grew dramatically. Train crews struggled to keep longer and heavier trains moving over the grades and curves of IC's main line south of Carbondale, Illinois. Between 1897 and 1902, a second main track was laid from Chicago to Fulton, Kentucky. The Cairo Bridge had also been strengthened to handle heavier motive power, but it was still a single-track structure. In spite of these improvements, the Centralia and Cairo districts were still the bottleneck of the Chicago-New Orleans main line.

Coincidentally, the Chicago, Burlington & Quincy was building a line from northern Illinois to the coal fields in the southern part of the state. The CB&Q was a railroad that stretched westward from Chicago across the plains to the Rocky Mountains. One of its most important routes reached up the Mississippi River to Minnesota's Twin Cities where the "Q" connected with the Great Northern and Northern Pacific. In 1901, the GN and NP purchased the CB&Q to secure a friendly connection to Chicago. GN's builder, northwestern rail magnate James J. Hill, was also wresting control of the NP with the intention of merging all three properties into a single railroad.

The Burlington reached far into southern Illinois for coal, not only as a source of fuel for its locomotives, but also as a commodity destined for residential and commercial consumption. In addition, interests on both sides of the Ohio River envisioned this new line to be part of a new route for rail traffic between the southeastern and northwestern states. The CB&Q built its southern Illinois line to Metropolis on the Ohio River. Plans for a bridge across the river and a line to Paducah were drawn up and a holding company, the Paducah & Illinois Railroad Company, was incorporated on February 21, 1910. The P&I would connect the CB&Q with the Nashville, Chattanooga & St. Louis at Paducah, Kentucky. Illinois Central participated in early stages of the bridge negotiations, but soon dropped out of the plan (as did Chicago & Eastern Illinois and New York Central's Big Four subsidiary).

OPPOSITE ABOVE: Northbound Illinois Central Gulf train CR-6 is about to pull onto the Champaign District from the Bluford District at Edgewood, Illinois, on April 15, 1988. This schedule handled traffic between Johnston Yard at Memphis and Champaign, Illinois, working at Fulton and Chiles, Kentucky, en route. The bulk of the traffic on CR-6 was destined for ICG's interchange with Conrail at Effingham. (Kirk Reynolds)

OPPOSITE BELOW: The conductor on a northbound Sahara Turn looks his train over as it pulls off the Edgewood Cutoff onto the Eldorado District at Rust Junction, Illinois, on October 21, 1989. Originating at Benton, Illinois, the train was loaded at Sahara Coal Company's mine on the Bluford District about 20 miles south of this junction. It is seen here returning to Benton. (Kirk Reynolds)

ABOVE: On October 22, 1989, northbound IC train NC-4 passes over US Route 45. Beyond the trees on the right, paralleling the road, was the right-of-way of New York Central's line to Cairo at Stonefort, Illinois. Southern Railway purchased the former NYC Cairo route in the late 1970s, and eventually abandoned it a few years later. (Kirk Reynolds)

OPPOSITE: The three tunnels on the Edgewood Cutoff are numbered from north to south. On a sunny October day in 1976, a southbound Illinois Central Gulf train emerges from Tunnel #2 at the prescribed speed limit of 25 miles per hour. The bore is the longest of three tunnels that were dug through the hills of the Shawnee National Forest. (Mike R. Schafer)

BELOW: On the afternoon of March 7, 1987, southbound CN-5 roars out of Tunnel #1 into the sunlight. The three tunnels were among the first locations where IC installed welded rail in the 1950s. For most people, this isn't a location that comes to mind when the Illinois Central is mentioned. (Greg C. Sieren)

The Illinois Central had already established itself in Paducah when it purchased the Chesapeake, Ohio & Southwestern in 1896. The CO&SW ran from Louisville to Memphis, crossing IC's Cairo-Jackson, Tennessee main line at Fulton, Kentucky. After IC took it over, the CO&SW was split into two distinct routes. South of Fulton, the CO&SW became part of IC's Chicago-New Orleans main line through Memphis. North of Fulton, the line became IC's Kentucky Division, reaching Louisville by way of Paducah.

IC had another, although somewhat circuitous, connection to Paducah from its main line. The Brookport District turned away from the main line at Carbondale and wandered southward through the woods to its namesake municipality on the north bank of the Ohio River. The carferry "W. B. Duncan" shuttled cars back and forth between Brookport and Paducah, but Illinois Central's management felt that there wasn't enough interchange traffic to justify its participation in a project as costly as the Metropolis bridge. However, traffic congestion on both sides of IC's own bridge at Cairo compelled those same directors to eventually take a second look at the new Metropolis bridge.

The solution to the problems at Cairo was to build a 168-mile freight bypass from Edgewood, Illinois, (on the Champaign District) to Fulton, Kentucky, that would cross the Ohio at Metropolis. The Edgewood Cutoff was laid out on a near north-south alignment and built much straighter than the Cairo route – so straight that the northernmost 63 miles of the line claims the title of longest stretch of straight track in Illinois. This new line would be 22 miles shorter than the main line between Edgewood and Fulton. Survey work began in 1916 and continued for eight years. On September 1, 1920, IC signed an agreement with the Paducah & Illinois' owners (CB&Q and NC&StL) that would allow the Cutoff to connect with the P&I at Metropolis so IC trains could cross the bridge. The Interstate Commerce Commission approved the deal in 1923 and construction crews went to work in 1925.

The Illinois portion of the line was built under the name of the Southern Illinois & Kentucky Railroad while the Kentucky side was part of the Chicago, St. Louis & New Orleans, the same IC subsidiary that owned the Cairo-New Orleans main line. The Kentucky end of the line began operation on April 7, 1927, and the Illinois side was completed on May 7, 1928. With the completion of the Cutoff, Illinois Central became the dominant partner of the Metropolis bridge, accounting for 75 percent of the traffic that moved across the structure.

In addition to the claim of the longest segment of tangent track in Illinois, the new line boasted another record in railway engineering achievements in the state. To keep the ruling grade of the Cutoff down to .03 percent, three tunnels were bored through the hills of Johnson and Pope counties, between 20 and 30 miles north of the Ohio River. The longest of the three bores was Tunnel Number 2, which measured 6,985 feet, making it the longest railroad tunnel in Illinois.

Operating authority on the Cutoff was divided between the Illinois and St. Louis divisions at Bluford, Illinois, roughly halfway

OPPOSITE ABOVE: The Edgewood Cutoff was built not only to expedite freight traffic between Chicago and Memphis, but also to give the Illinois Central access to coal mines along the line in southern Illinois. A southbound IC coal train is about to pass beneath Illinois State Route 147 at Robbs, Illinois, on October 22, 1989. (Kirk Reynolds)

OPPOSITE BELOW: Southbound Illinois Central Gulf train CN-5 (a Chicago-New Orleans freight schedule) breaks into the sunlight as it exits the south portal of Tunnel #3 on December 13, 1986. This is the southernmost of the tunnels on the cutoff, situated less than 20 miles north of the Ohio River. (Greg C. Sieren)

ABOVE: On February 27, 1988, Illinois Central Gulf train CR-5 passes a northbound grain train as it rolls beneath the coal dock at Reevesville, Illinois. Robustly built to serve the largest steam locomotives operated by the Illinois Central (such as the 2500 and 2600 class 4-8-2s), the tower still stands decades after the last steam locomotives were retired. (Greg C. Sieren)

between Champaign and Fulton. The north 40 miles of the Cutoff was designated the Edgewood Line of the Champaign District. The movement of trains on this segment was governed by the dispatcher at Champaign. The line south of Bluford was designated the Bluford District. Operations on this district were governed by the dispatcher located in St. Louis Division headquarters at Carbondale, Illinois. A yard and engine servicing facility at Bluford served as the terminal for crews operating trains from Champaign, Fulton and Paducah.

When built, the Edgewood Cutoff was equipped with automatic block signals. A Centralized Traffic Control (CTC) system was installed between Bluford and Fulton, Kentucky, in 1961. The dispatcher at the St. Louis Division offices in Carbondale operated the CTC machine until Illinois Central consolidated its dispatching operations at its Chicago headquarters in the late 1960s.

Compared to most of Illinois, the rural southern region (sometimes referred to as "Little Egypt") that the Cutoff was projected through was relatively devoid of railroads. The line crossed four foreign railroads, none at grade. It passed under three; B&O's (later Chessie System, then CSX) Cincinnati-St. Louis main line at Greendale, Southern's (now Norfolk Southern) Louisville-St. Louis route at Bluford and L&N's (also CSX) St. Louis line at Belle Rive. The Bluford District passed over the New York Central subsidiary Big Four's line to Cairo at Stonefort. The line also passed over a New York Central branch to a coal mine at Allenby. Since Illinois Central built the Cutoff as a thoroughfare for expediting freight traffic, no interchange with other railroads (north of Metropolis) was incorporated into its construction.

The centerpiece of the Edgewood Cutoff is the impressive Metropolis bridge and its associated trackage, the Paducah &

Illinois Railroad. The northern end of the P&I connected with the Chicago, Burlington & Quincy Railroad, which became part of Burlington Northern in 1970 and is now BNSF Railway, at Burlington Junction. A mile south of that point, the Bluford Subdivision meets the P&I at Metropolis Junction, a short distance from the north end of the bridge. On the Kentucky side of the river, the Paducah & Illinois turns east toward Paducah and the Cutoff continues south at Chiles Junction. Paducah was the southern gateway to the Kentucky Division, Illinois Central's route to Louisville. Illinois Central Gulf sold the Kentucky Division to CG&T Industries on August 27, 1986, and line became the Paducah & Louisville Railway (PAL). The Paducah & Illinois

Railroad is now jointly owned by three railroads: Canadian National, BNSF and Paducah & Louisville.

The southern end of the Edgewood Cutoff was New Yard, located at Fulton, Kentucky, 42.5 miles south of Chiles Junction. The Bluford District crossed the Cairo District north of town at Bluford Crossing. There were connecting tracks on three sides of the crossing that allowed the movement of trains between the two districts. The majority of train schedules operating over the cutoff were Chicago-Memphis trains and many were scheduled to pick up and set out cars at New Yard. The south end of the yard connected with the Fulton District, the former CO&SW line to Memphis, at Oaks, Tennessee.

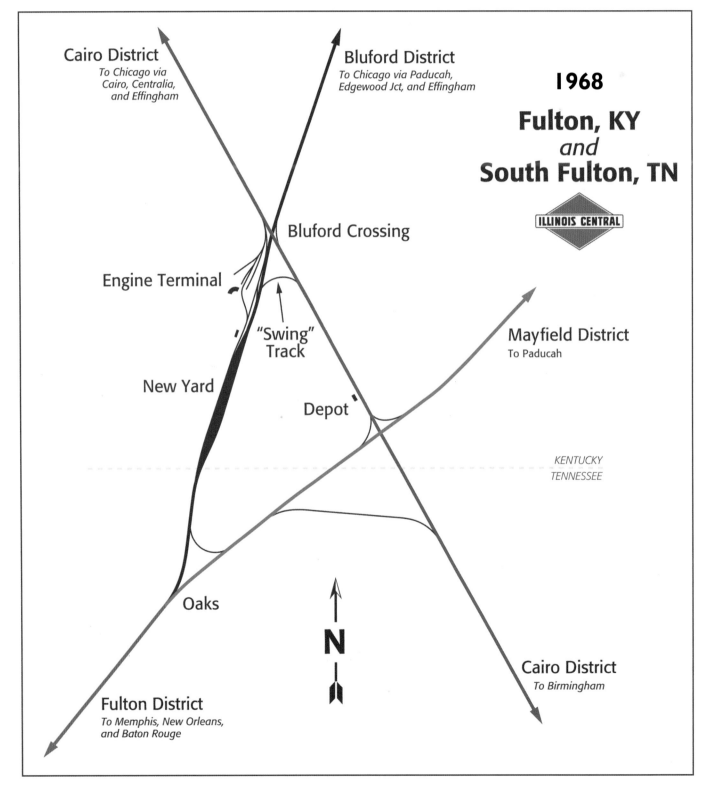

TOP: On May 28, 1989, a northbound train of empty coal hoppers led by a pair of SD40s that were built for the Gulf, Mobile & Ohio in 1966 passes over the Illinois shore of the Ohio River on the P&I bridge at Metropolis, Illinois. (Scott D. Lindsey)

ABOVE: Several deep cuts were excavated during the construction of the Kentucky segment of the cutoff. Southbound grain train RGA-314 passes through one of these cuts near Fulgham, Kentucky, on February 15, 1986. Some of the material from these cuts was moved to Paducah and used as fill during the construction of IC's new locomotive shop. (Bill E. Dressler)

Eldorado District

For much of the 20th century, Illinois Central and other railroads operated a network of branch lines in southern Illinois to reach the numerous coal mines in the area. Extending across Perry, Franklin and Saline counties, IC's Eldorado District provided access to several mine branches and served as a link between the main line at Du Quoin and the Bluford District. When IC rebuilt its bridge at Cairo between 1950 and 1952, mainline traffic was temporarily rerouted to the Metropolis bridge by way of the Eldorado District.

The Eldorado District was actually comprised of two separate segments: a 30-mile section running between the main line and the Edgewood Cutoff and a shorter branch that ran eastward from the cutoff. The longer segment of the district crossed two other railroads. The Chicago, Burlington & Quincy's line to the bridge at Metropolis was intersected at Christopher, seven miles from Du Quoin. At Benton, eight miles east of Christopher, the district crossed the Chicago & Eastern Illinois main line. The C&EI route through southern Illinois was acquired by Missouri Pacific in 1967 and became part of MP's Chicago-Texas main line. The MP merged with Union Pacific in 1982.

OPPOSITE ABOVE: On August 18, 1985, the engine consist on southbound Chicago-New Orleans manifest freight CN-5 has been cut off the train and is about to cross the Cairo District at Bluford Crossing as it heads for Fulton's New Yard to make a pick-up. A pair of gates (that were operated by controls in the box on the other side of the track) provided protection on the Bluford District side of the crossing, while the Cairo District side was protected by signals. (Scott D. Lindsey)

OPPOSITE BELOW: Northbound Memphis-Chicago train MCH rolls across the former IC Cairo District as it departs Fulton on April 29, 1990. Illinois Central had sold the Cairo District south of Bluford Crossing, the former GM&O route between Jackson, Tennessee and Corinth, Mississippi, and the Birmingham District to Norfolk Southern in the summer of 1988. (Kirk Reynolds)

ABOVE: An Illinois Central mine run pulls past the former CB&Q depot at Sesser, Illinois, on October 18, 1991, as it leaves Old Ben mine #26. The mine was operated by Zeigler Coal Company and was served by Illinois Central and Burlington Northern. This train continued southward on the BN for a couple of miles to reach a connecting track at Valier where it returned to IC rails. (Kirk Reynolds)

OPPOSITE ABOVE: The compact engine servicing facility at Benton, Illinois, provided fuel, sand and routine maintenance for locomotives that powered Illinois Central and Illinois Central Gulf coal trains. While the majority of these units were six-motor locomotives, an exception to the norm reposed at Benton on the morning of June 12, 1988. GP11 #8731 and an unidentified GP38 were being prepared for their return to Carbondale on the Carbondale-Benton Turn. (Kirk Reynolds)

OPPOSITE BELOW: The Eldorado District crossed Union Pacific's (former MP/C&EI) bustling Chicago Subdivision at Benton. A gate interlocked with the home signals of both railroads protected this crossing and was normally aligned for the UP main. When an Illinois Central train approached the crossing, a clerk from the nearby IC yard office would drive to the crossing and line the gate for the IC train to cross. After the Illinois Central train cleared the crossing, the clerk would swing the gate back across the Eldorado District. On October 21, 1989, this short IC train crossed the Union Pacific main with four cars to be handed over to the UP. (Kirk Reynolds)

ABOVE: A trio of SD40s with a train of empty hoppers headed eastward on the Eldorado District west of Akin, Illinois, on March 26, 1988. At Rust Junction, this train turned south onto the Bluford District on its way to be loaded at one of the mines served by the Illinois Central. (R. M. Leach)

In the heyday of the southern Illinois coal mining industry, Illinois Central, Chicago Burlington & Quincy and Chicago & Eastern Illinois worked together to move coal from the mines to markets around the region. Some of the coal mines were served jointly by more than one railroad. In the 1960s, coal producers and railroads initiated the movement of coal in dedicated trains destined for a single customer, mainly electric utilities and steel makers. New federal air pollution laws were passed during the 1970s that restricted use of much of the coal produced in southern Illinois due to its high sulfur content. As the strict Clean Air Act

Amendments of 1990 went into effect, many of the coal mines closed and most of the web of feeder lines that served these mines were abandoned.

Most of the Illinois Central mine runs that served the coal loaders east of the main line operated out of Benton, Illinois. Crews for these runs were based at Benton and power for the coal trains was serviced at the yard's refueling facility. Generally, a train was operated to the mine as a turn, and would be returned loaded to Benton where a road crew would take it either to an on-line customer or for interchange with another railroad.

BELOW: A grain train turns northward from the Eldorado District onto the Edgewood Cutoff on October 28, 1989. The north leg of the wye at the eastern end of the Eldorado District was designated Akin Junction while the south connection (which the photographer was standing next to when this photo was taken) was called Rust Junction. (Kirk Reynolds)

OPPOSITE: Northbound Birmingham-Chicago train BC-4 was once one of the hottest trains on the railroad, heavy with produce traffic from the southeast. The schedule survived into the ICG era and is seen pulling onto the single main track at Buda, Kentucky, just north of Fulton on the evening of May 14, 1988. Instead of fruit and vegetables, the train had become a mix of woodchip hoppers, pulpwood on bulkhead flats and what appears to be coal or coke in hoppers. (Greg C. Sieren)

The Cairo District - North End

Reaching southward from Illinois Central's bridge across the Ohio River, the Cairo District constituted a fundamental segment of the railroad's Chicago-New Orleans main line. When constructed in 1873 as the Mississippi Central's Cairo extension, the new line brought the northern terminal of that road from Jackson, Tennessee, to East Cairo, Kentucky. For the next 20 years, Illinois Central's New Orleans traffic moved over the MC by way of Jackson, Tennessee, and Water Valley Junction, Mississippi, bypassing Memphis.

The Mississippi Central & Tennessee was the first railroad to reach Jackson, Tennessee, completed in May, 1858. The Mobile & Ohio arrived in Jackson six months later. The M&O provided the MC&T with a connection to steamboats on the Mississippi River at Columbus, Kentucky, which, in turn, made it possible for passengers and freight to reach the southern terminus of the Illinois Central at Cairo. The Mississippi Central & Tennessee was absorbed by the Mississippi Central in 1859 and the interchange of traffic with the M&O at Jackson continued until hostilities between the northern and southern states curtailed regular railroad operations in 1861.

After the war, the Mississippi Central and its connection to New Orleans, the New Orleans, Jackson & Great Northern, were drawn into Illinois Central's sphere of influence. The MC had revived its interchange with the Mobile & Ohio at Jackson and Illinois Central management initially hoped it would be able to induce the M&O to build a line from Columbus to a point across the Ohio River from Cairo. But the M&O was destitute, so the IC provided funding to the MC that enabled it to lay its own track to East Cairo. The M&O eventually extended its line from Columbus to East Cairo in 1882.

The broad gauge Mississippi Central came under direct control of the Illinois Central in 1877 and was integrated into IC subsidiary Chicago, St. Louis & New Orleans. Under its new owner, the amount of traffic on the former Mississippi Central route began to increase. The subsequent conversion of the MC's track gauge from five feet to standard gauge (carried out in the summer of 1881) was a crucial step in bringing Illinois Central's southern lines into conformance with the rest of the railroad. The completion of the bridge over the Ohio River in 1889 melded the CStL&NO into the Chicago-New Orleans trunk line and the section between the bridge and Jackson, Tennessee, became Illinois Central's Cairo District.

ABOVE: On April 29, 1990, northbound Illinois Central train MES (Memphis-East St. Louis) slides through a cut north of Arlington, Kentucky, about 20 miles north of Fulton. This was one of the sections of the Cairo District on which centralized traffic control allowed the elimination of the second main track, reducing maintenance expenses while continuing to move traffic efficiently. The Cairo District was one of two CTC projects that the IC completed in 1962; the other controlled ten miles of the Dubuque District between Freeport and Lena, Illinois. (Kirk Reynolds)

Concurrently, Illinois Central had assembled a network of lines in northwestern Mississippi that extended southward from Memphis. One of these lines connected Memphis with Illinois Central's main line at Grenada, Mississippi, but IC had no route to Memphis from the north. The 1896 purchase of the Chesapeake, Ohio & Southwestern gave Illinois Central its northern approach to Memphis. The Cairo District crossed the CO&SW at Fulton, Kentucky, a small town on the Kentucky-Tennessee state line. Fulton quickly became one of the IC's busiest junctions.

In 1886, the Mobile & Ohio's influence reached across the Ohio River when it took control of a line between Cairo and East St. Louis. To connect its lines on both sides of the Ohio River, the M&O negotiated a trackage rights agreement with the IC in 1899, allowing the passage of its trains over the bridge between Ballard, Kentucky, (at the southern end of the bridge) and Cairo. The M&O operated a track that paralleled the IC between Ballard and Winford Junction and an arrangement was made so each railroad could operate its trains over the tracks of the other. This agreement remained in effect after the M&O merged with the Gulf, Mobile & Northern in 1940 to form the Gulf, Mobile & Ohio. Following the 1972 ICG merger, the former GM&O line south of Winford Junction was abandoned.

To ease traffic congestion at the Cairo bridge, Illinois Central constructed the Edgewood Cutoff in the 1920s. The new freight line paralleled the Centralia and Cairo districts and tied into the main line to Memphis at Fulton. Most of the Chicago-Memphis freight trains were rerouted over the Cutoff while all the passenger trains continued to run on the main line and over the Cairo bridge.

In 1962, a centralized traffic control (CTC) system was installed on the Cairo District between the north end of the Ohio River bridge (which is designated Illinois) and Fulton. One main track was removed and two passing sidings were put in service at Bardwell and Clinton, Kentucky. Upon completion of the project, the north end of the Cairo District was moved from Ballard to North Cairo. The new CTC machine that controlled traffic between Cairo and Fulton was placed in the St. Louis Division dispatcher's offices at Carbondale, Illinois. Prior to the installation of centralized traffic control, the movement of trains on the entire Cairo District had been governed by the dispatcher located at Jackson, Tennessee.

Fulton - Illinois Central's Crossroads

Five IC main lines converged at a pair of small towns that straddled the Kentucky-Tennessee border: Fulton, Kentucky, and South Fulton, Tennessee. The Cairo District ran straight through Fulton on its way to Jackson, Tennessee. It crossed the Bluford District (the Edgewood Cutoff) at Bluford Crossing north of town and the Mayfield District (part of the old C&OSW main line that came in from Paducah) near Fulton's business district. South of Bluford Crossing, the Edgewood Cutoff rolled into New Yard, which was built to replace the original MC and C&OSW yards in town. Many IC freight schedules were coordinated through this facility, which stretched between Bluford Crossing and Oaks, where the Mayfield and Fulton districts met. The Fulton District was the main line to Memphis that ran southwest from South Fulton.

Depending on the specific train schedule, traffic on the Cairo District could go three different directions at Fulton. Passenger trains continued on the Cairo District through Bluford Crossing to the passenger depot in downtown Fulton. The Mayfield District crossed the Cairo District just south of the depot at Fulton Junction. Passenger trains to and from Memphis would use a connection track that steered them between the Mayfield and Cairo Districts. Sometimes, freight trains that didn't have work to do at the yard would also use this route. The Chicago-Florida passenger trains and Birmingham freight proceeded on the Cairo District to Jackson, Tennessee.

After the Illinois Central Gulf merger, the number of trains operating over the Mayfield District declined. As the railroad pursued a program to cast off numerous lines in the early 1980s, it petitioned the Interstate Commerce Commission for permission to abandon the Mayfield District north of Fulton. Permission was granted and the southern end of the district between Fulton and Clayburn, Kentucky, was torn up in 1983.

In the summer of 1988, as IC Industries prepared to spin off the Illinois Central Gulf, the Cairo District south of Fulton disappeared from ICG's map. Norfolk Southern purchased the former IC route to Birmingham on June 26, 1988, to create a shorter route for its St. Louis-Sheffield, Alabama traffic. Trackage rights over ICG's Cairo District north of Fulton and the Centralia District between Cairo and Centralia, Illinois, were included in the deal. Initially, NS ran four trains a day (two in each direction) through Fulton.

When the newly independent IC under Edward Moyers reconfigured the main line as a single-track railroad and IC's traffic increased, NS trains operating over the Centralia District encountered numerous delays. These impediments eventually prompted NS management's decision to stop running its trains over the IC. By that time, all IC trains on the Cairo District (including Amtrak trains #58 and #59, the "City of New Orleans") were operating around the connection at Bluford Crossing and through, or past, New Yard. The diamond at Bluford Crossing was removed in the mid-1990s and the north end of the yard became Cairo Junction.

Passenger Service through Fulton

During the 1960s, passenger operations on most of America's railroads were in varying degrees of decline, but Illinois Central's defied the trend. Few other executives in the industry at the time were as dedicated to providing quality passenger service as Wayne Johnston. Though passenger revenue had fallen during the 1950s, IC's passenger trains continued to be a source of pride for the railroad's management and employees and remained among the best in the nation.

There were four pairs of passenger schedules running between Chicago and New Orleans in the early 1960s. Leading the pack were the standard-bearers of the railroad's passenger fleet; the all-Pullman "Panama Limited" (trains #5 and #6) and its all-

ABOVE: Northbound train BC-4 has stopped north of Bluford Crossing as it prepares to make its set-off at Fulton Yard on May 7, 1988. The rows of streetlights next to the tracks are for the illumination of a fueling station that Illinois Central Gulf set up on the Cairo District so trains that didn't work the yard could be refueled without cutting the power from the train. The small building to the right of the other track is Amtrak's Fulton station. (Scott D. Lindsey)

coach counterpart, the "City of New Orleans" (trains #1 and #2). Next in rank was the "Louisiane" (trains #3 and #4), which was made up of a mix of coaches and sleepers. Rounding out the fleet was the southbound "Southern Express" (train #25) and its northbound partner, the "Creole" (train #8).

In addition to the New Orleans varnish, three other passenger schedules ran through Fulton. The "Chickasaw" was a secondary mail and express train that operated every day between St. Louis and Memphis. The "Chickasaw" also handled Pullman cars for the "Panama Limited" between St. Louis and Carbondale. In the Chicago-Florida market, Illinois Central was represented by the every-other-day streamliner "City of Miami" and the daily "Seminole." Altogether, 11 passenger trains made their scheduled stop at Fulton's venerable wood frame depot every day. Some of the trains occasionally operated with extra sections, especially during the holiday season.

In spite of the railroad's best efforts, patronage on its passenger trains stagnated as operating costs continued to rise. Through the 1960s, as the interstate highway system expanded and airlines improved their service, more people were driving or flying to their destinations. As strong an advocate as Wayne Johnston was for IC's passenger trains, he was a pragmatist. His principal obligation was to the shareholders, who were more interested in share price and dividends than the railroad's public image. Johnston retired as the railroad's president in May 1966 and the job of reconfiguring the railroad's passenger train business was left to his successor.

When William B. Johnson brought aboard Paul Reistrup as vice president of Illinois Central's Passenger Service Department in 1967, the winds of change were already blowing. On March 11, 1967, a number of IC's passenger schedules were revised. Southbound train #25, "Southern Express" was cut back to a Chicago-Carbondale run and renamed the "Campus" (train #28

BELOW: It's June 1975, almost three years after the Illinois Central Gulf merger, but this scene at Fulton's New Yard certainly appears to be at a Gulf, Mobile & Ohio facility before the union. The two units, GM&O #714 and 754, will become ICG #9533 and 9574, respectively. The GP38 #9533 was sold, but GP38-2 #9574 was still an active unit on the Canadian National two decades after the IC/CN merger. (Steve H. Forrest)

OPPOSITE ABOVE: During the steam era, the roundhouse at Fulton provided for the refueling and servicing of road power that ran between Centralia, Bluford, Paducah and Memphis as well as engines that ran on local freights based at Fulton. With the advent of the diesel, the engines on some road freights were refueled at Fulton while other schedules passed through without stopping or stopped only to pick up and set out cars. A lone GP10 was parked by the turntable as a set of road power was being serviced at the Fulton engine house on July 14, 1985. (Scott D. Lindsey)

OPPOSITE BELOW: Though diesel locomotives required far less maintenance than steam locomotives, they still needed fuel, sand and inspection and those services continued after the Fulton roundhouse closed. The hostler at Fulton is getting ready to return this pair of GP9s back to service and has just finished filling the sandbox on #9063 on this April afternoon in 1968. (Morgan McIlwain)

ABOVE: The station agent stands ready to load baggage as Illinois Central train #4, the "Mid-American," glides to a stop at Dyersburg, Tennessee, in September 1970. This massive depot burned down in the late 1970s, leaving Amtrak riders using this stop with no shelter. In 1992, Amtrak moved this stop nine miles north to the smaller town of Newbern. The town's brick IC passenger station had been restored by local volunteers with the support of the municipal government and was designated the Dyersburg-Newbern stop for trains #58/59, the "City of New Orleans." (David M. Johnston)

was the northbound "Campus") and the northbound "Creole" (train #8) was reduced to a New Orleans-Memphis accommodation. Also on that date, the "Chickasaw" stopped running south of Carbondale, Illinois, and the northbound "Louisiane" was pared to a schedule that ran between Memphis and Chicago.

A more thorough transformation of Illinois Central's passenger services began the following October. A new schedule was added to IC's passenger train line-up; the "Magnolia Star." Though listed separately in Illinois Central's public timetable, the "Magnolia Star" was simply the addition of some coaches and a café-lounge to the heretofore all-Pullman "Panama Limited." The short-lived "Star" was dropped from the timetable in December 1968, but the coaches remained part of the "Panama's" consist.

In December, train #3, the southbound "Louisiane," was discontinued south of Memphis and the remaining train and its northbound counterpart (train #4) were renamed the "Mid-American." The New Orleans-Memphis "Creole" (train #8) was also discontinued. The new "Mid-American" continued to carry the "Chickasaw's" coaches between Carbondale and Memphis.

As the 1960s came to an end, passenger traffic through Fulton continued to fade. Illinois Central's passenger department was concentrating its assets in the Chicago-Carbondale "Mini-Corridor," where students enrolled at the University of Illinois at Champaign-Urbana and Southern Illinois University at Carbondale provided a strong traffic base for IC passenger trains. On June 3, 1969, the railroad discontinued the "Seminole" south of Carbondale and dubbed the surviving train the "Shawnee," leav-

ing only the "City of Miami" to serve what remained of the once-lucrative Florida market.

Through 1970, Congress and the White House worked to relieve the nation's railroads of the burden of providing unprofitable passenger service by creating the National Railroad Passenger Corporation, initially called Railpax. The new agency would take over the operation of the passenger trains of the railroads that joined the system, keeping some routes and discontinuing others to create a national rail passenger network. Illinois Central would sign on to the new system along with 19 other lines. As the legislation to establish the NRPC was being worked out, IC's "Mid-American" was truncated to a Chicago-Carbondale train on September 15, 1970.

In late April 1971, Railpax officially became Amtrak and the federal agency took over the passenger services of the member railroads on May 1. In many cases, the new operator continued to run existing passenger schedules as part of its new national system, but a number of trains that were not included in Amtrak's network were discontinued. In Illinois Central's case, the "City of New Orleans" and the "Shawnee" became Amtrak trains while all other IC intercity passenger services were discontinued.

As Amtrak trains #58 and #59, the "City" went through something of an identity crisis. The train's name was changed to the "Panama Limited" in November 1971 only to have the former title restored in 1981. Amtrak moved out of Illinois Central's passenger depot near downtown Fulton to its own pre-fabricated structure north of town in 1979.

Freight Operations through Fulton

In the scheme of Illinois Central freight schedules, few places figured as prominently as Fulton and South Fulton. All the manifest freight schedules that operated between IC's major terminals in the upper Midwest (Chicago and East St. Louis in particular) and those in the southern states (New Orleans, Birmingham and Jackson, Mississippi) passed through Fulton. Many of these trains paused at Fulton to pick up and set out blocks of cars and to change crews.

One distinctive commodity that the Illinois Central handled for decades was the banana trade. This traffic was expedited northward in solid trains of refrigerator cars that ran on tight schedules. To preserve the quality of the tropical fruit, the temperature inside the refrigerator cars had to be carefully controlled. When a banana train arrived at Fulton, it stopped at the icing platform that stood along the east side of New Yard. In the summer, the ice in each car was topped off. During the winter, charcoal heaters were placed in the cars to prevent the yellow cargo from freezing.

In recognition of the banana traffic that passed through Fulton and South Fulton, the local citizenry organized an annual banana festival in 1962. In addition to the Grand Parade and the crowning of the Banana Princess, the event also featured the annual creation of a batch of banana pudding that weighed a full ton. Ironically, the festival was founded at a time when refrigerated trucks were taking the banana business away from the railroad.

IC's shipments of the fruit fell from thousands of carloads per month in the 1950s to less than 400 carloads for the entire year of 1971. By the end of the 1970s, the banana traffic was gone.

As the banana traffic diminished, a new source of revenue came on the scene. In the 1950s, railroads were experimenting with hauling truck trailers on flat cars. Recognizing the potential of this new market, Illinois Central inaugurated its own intermodal service in June 1955. Initially, this piggyback traffic was handled on dispatch freight trains between Chicago and Memphis. The following year, the service was extended to New Orleans and St. Louis. The trailer-on-flatcar business grew steadily as new loading ramps began operating at several locations along the IC, including Birmingham and Jackson, Mississippi.

In 1961, IC's dispatch freight schedules operating through Fulton were covered by the following trains:

Southbound

CN-1	Chicago (Markham Yard)-New Orleans
CN-5	Chicago (Congress Street Yard)-New Orleans
CB-9	Chicago (Markham Yard)-Birmingham
SE-1	Chicago (Congress Street Yard)-Birmingham
SN-3	St. Louis-New Orleans
SM-1	St. Louis-Memphis
LM-3	Louisville-Memphis

ABOVE: Illinois Central Gulf caboose #199698 protects the rear of southbound train SM-3 (East St. Louis-Memphis) as it rolls past the yard office at Dyersburg on August 18, 1985. Behind the depot is IC's Hickman District. The branch was sold by ICG in 1983 and became the Tennken Railroad. (Scott D. Lindsey)

Northbound

NC-2	New Orleans-Chicago (Congress Street Yard)
NC-6	New Orleans-Chicago (Congress Street Yard)
BC-2	Birmingham-Chicago (Markham Yard)
BC-4	Birmingham-Chicago (Congress Street Yard)
MI-2	Memphis-Indianapolis
MS-2	Memphis-St. Louis
ML-2	Memphis-Louisville

In July 1968, a pair of dedicated piggyback schedules (trains #50 and #51) began running between Chicago and Memphis. The trains were initially pulled by E-units that had been made surplus by cuts in passenger services, but as intermodal traffic increased and trains grew longer, the passenger engines soon proved to be inadequate for the job. Trios of GP40s became the standard power for the TOFC trains. To emphasize their swift pace, Illinois Central's marketing department branded the railroad's piggyback trains "Fastbacks" (a contraction of the term fast piggyback) and developed a "pig-on-wheels" logo to adorn their trailers. In addition to trailers, the "Fastbacks" also handled loaded autorack cars destined for IC's automobile unloading facilities at Memphis and Jackson, Mississippi.

Also in 1968, Illinois Central introduced its Rent-A-Train program, marking the railroad's entry into unit grain train operations. In October of that year, grain merchandiser Cargill, Inc. became the first shipper to use the new service. Over the next three decades, the bulk movement of grain became a staple of Illinois Central's and Illinois Central Gulf's revenue base.

After Illinois Central merged with GM&O in 1972, new traffic patterns began to evolve. Freight schedules through Fulton changed gradually as traffic that had previously been routed via GM&O was moved to former IC lines. In the late 1970s, ICG extended intermodal train #51's schedule to New Orleans and added another pig train (#53) between Chicago and Jackson, Mississippi. In 1977, five years after the merger, the line-up of manifest and intermodal schedules operating through Fulton was made up of the following trains:

Southbound

CM-1	Chicago-Memphis
CM-7	Chicago-Memphis
CN-5	Chicago-New Orleans
SE-1	Chicago-Birmingham
CB-1	Chicago-Birmingham
SLX	Kansas City-Jackson, Tennessee
MFB	Memphis-Birmingham
IM-1	Indianapolis-Memphis
SM-3	East St. Louis-Memphis
SM-5	East St. Louis-Memphis
LM-1	Louisville-Memphis
LM-7	Louisville-Memphis
51	Chicago IMX (Intermodal Exchange)-New Orleans
53	Chicago IMX-Jackson, Mississippi

Northbound

NC-6	New Orleans-Chicago
GC-6	Geismar-Chicago
GS-2	Geismar-St. Louis
BC-2	Birmingham-Chicago
BC-4	Birmingham-Chicago
WLX	Jackson, Tennessee-Kansas City
JFM	Jackson, Tennessee-Memphis
MC-4	Memphis-Chicago
MS-2	Memphis-East St. Louis
MI-2	Memphis-Indianapolis
ML-2	Memphis-Louisville
ML-4	Memphis-Louisville
BC-4	Birmingham-Chicago
50	New Orleans-Chicago IMX
52	Memphis-Chicago IMX

As Illinois Central Gulf sold off large portions of its system in the 1980s, its train schedules were also trimmed down. In addition to these scheduled trains, ICG also ran unscheduled manifest trains, which were referred to as "dead freights." The following list of freight schedules reflects the reduced traffic levels passing through Fulton in 1987:

Southbound

CN-5	Chicago-New Orleans
CM-1	Chicago-Memphis
SE-1	Chicago-Birmingham
CR-5	Champaign, IL-Memphis
SM-3	East St. Louis-Memphis
51	Chicago IMX-New Orleans

Northbound

NC-6	New Orleans-Chicago
MC-4	Memphis-Chicago
BC-4	Birmingham-Chicago
GS-2	Geismar, Louisiana-East St. Louis
CR-6	Memphis-Champaign, Illinois
50	New Orleans-Chicago IMX

After IC Industries spun the railroad off in 1989, the "new" Illinois Central's operating department reworked its train symbols. A three-letter alpha code that was initially employed was modified to a four-letter code when a new computer system was installed in 1990. Train symbols for manifest freights were assigned a two-letter code for both originating and final terminals. Intermodal trains received a simple "I" prefix that was followed by two digits to identify the train's schedule.

OPPOSITE: Southbound train CN-5 (Chicago-New Orleans) seems to part a sea of vegetation as it rolls through the massive cut at Ripley, Tennessee, on May 27, 1988. The hillside in the foreground is covered with kudzu, a vine native to Asia that can be found across the southeastern third of the continental United States. Brought to this country in the late 19th century, kudzu became a regional legend in southern states after programs to use it in the 1930 and 1940s for erosion control greatly expanded its presence. Due to kudzu's aggressive nature, it could dominate in areas where it wasn't managed and many northern visitors would return home with tall tales of the vine's exaggerated abilities. The train's engine consist is one that could only be found on the ICG; the lead unit is SD40A #6011, the middle unit SD28 #9450 and the trailing unit is SD20 #2036. The SD40A and the SD20 were models operated exclusively by the ICG. Only one other railroad owned SD28s and it was an iron-ore line in Minnesota. (Kirk Reynolds)

In 1997, Illinois Central's manifest freight and intermodal schedules through Fulton are as follows:

Southbound

CHME Chicago (Markham)-Memphis
GLME Chicago (Glenn)-Memphis
GLNO Chicago (Glenn)-New Orleans
CRME Effingham-Memphis
ESME East St. Louis-Memphis
I01   Chicago MIT*-New Orleans
I03   Chicago MIT*-Memphis
I07   East St. Louis-Memphis

Northbound

MECH Memphis-Chicago
MECR Memphis-Effingham
MEES Memphis-East St. Louis
I02   New Orleans-Chicago MIT*
I04   New Orleans-Chicago MIT*
I14   Memphis-Chicago MIT*

*Moyers Intermodal Terminal

Following IC's 1999 merger with Canadian National, train symbols were converted to fit into CN's numerical train symbol system.

The Fulton District

Stretching 110 miles across the very western end of Tennessee, the Fulton District linked the cities of Fulton and Memphis. Every one of Illinois Central's premier Chicago-New Orleans passenger trains (that often included second sections), as well as dozens of freight movements, were funneled over the IC's Fulton District every day.

While the public timetable maps depicted the Fulton District as double-track the entire distance between Fulton and Memphis, Tennessee, there were actually four locations where the double track was reduced to single track in order to cross river bridges. Spring switches were employed where double track went to single. The single-track sections were at Obion over the Obion River, South Dyersburg over the Forked Deer River, Mill Creek over the South Fork of the Forked Deer River and Rialto over the Big Hatchie River.

Another unique feature of the Fulton District was the main-line sidings, which were located between the two main tracks. These were an engineering hallmark of the era when E. H. Harriman controlled the Illinois Central.

Illinois Central was the dominant railroad in western Tennessee and the Fulton District met two other railroads at three locations between Fulton and Memphis. A Louisville & Nashville branch that ran from Bruceton to Union City, Tennessee, crossed the Fulton District at Gibbs. The L&N line had been a branch of the Nashville, Chattanooga & St. Louis Railway that went to Hickman, Kentucky, until 1951, when the NC&StL abandoned it west of Union City. After the L&N absorbed the NC&StL in 1957, it continued to operate the branch. L&N became part of Seaboard System Railroad in 1982 and the branch through Gibbs was abandoned soon afterward.

The Fulton District encountered the Gulf, Mobile & Ohio Railroad at two places. The former Mobile & Ohio mainline intersected the Fulton District at Rives, mile 284. Following the ICG merger, the GM&O main was downgraded to local service and most of it was abandoned or sold to short line railroads. Illinois Central Gulf retained about 4.5 miles of the old M&O between Rives and Union City and incorporated it into the Fulton District in 1982. The other GM&O line connected with IC's main line at Dyersburg, mile 314. This was the former Gulf, Mobile & Northern that ran between Dyersburg and Jackson, Tennessee. With the exception of short sections of track at Dyersburg and Jackson, the line was torn up after 1977.

ABOVE: On November 10, 1973, this southbound train rolled down the Fulton District through Millington, Tennessee, led by IC #9046. This engine was part of a six-unit order of GP9s equipped with steam generators for passenger service that were delivered in May 1954. Apparently the 9046's battery box doors got switched with those from a GP7 at some point. IC GP7s were numbered 8800-8981 while GP9s were 9000-9389. (David M. Johnston)

BELOW: Southbound train LM-7 (Louisville-Memphis) passes the yard office at Woodstock, Tennessee, on December 8, 1985, and is about to take the switch that will guide it onto IC's belt line around the eastern edge of Memphis to reach its destination, Johnston Yard. The double-track bypass from Woodstock to East Junction was built by the IC between 1905 and 1908 to expedite the movement of through freight traffic around the city by avoiding the congestion of the original riverfront route. By the early 1990s, all freight trains were routed over the belt line with the exception of a local based at Woodstock that switched the remaining industry on the city line. (Scott D. Lindsey)

Only one branch diverged from the Fulton-Memphis main line. The Hickman District reached northward about 52 miles from Dyersburg to Hickman, Kentucky. Illinois Central Gulf sold the entire district to the Hickman River City Development Corporation in September 1983 and the line has since been operated by the Tennken Railroad.

The southern end of the Fulton District met the Memphis Terminal District at Woodstock, Tennessee, mile 380, about 11 miles north of downtown Memphis. The IC main line split at Woodstock to form two routes; one through the city and other around it. Passenger trains took the former CO&SW main line through town while most freight traffic went around Memphis on the belt route. A yard south of the junction at Woodstock handled traffic for a nearby chemical plant.

ABOVE: The Kentucky Derby, which is run at Louisville's Churchill Downs, is America's (if not the world's) best-known horse race. Traditionally run on the first Saturday in May, it draws spectators from around the world. In the halcyon days of rail travel, every railroad that served Louisville operated at least one Derby Special (some roads ran several) every year. A southbound Derby special paused at Oak Street Yard in May 1965 as the road locomotives were put on the train. A switch engine had pulled the special from its parking spot near downtown. (Charles B. Castner)

Of the five states that Illinois Central's Chicago-New Orleans route passed through, only 45 miles of the entire main line were located in the commonwealth of Kentucky. On the other hand, the IC's biggest presence in the Bluegrass State was its secondary main line to Louisville (and associated branches), which was appropriately named the Kentucky Division. The Kentucky Division played a dual role for Illinois Central. It provided the Louisville connection for IC's mainline passenger trains, as well as the freight traffic that was interchanged with the northeastern trunk lines that served the city. The Kentucky Division was also the prevalent railroad in western Kentucky's coal-mining region.

Strung across the hills of the lower Ohio Valley, the backbone of the Kentucky Division was the former Chesapeake, Ohio & Southwestern from Louisville to Fulton, Kentucky. Illinois Central divided the 270-mile main line into three districts: the Louisville, Paducah and Mayfield Districts. The Evansville, Uniontown, Providence, Owensboro, Hodgenville and East Cairo Districts made up the branch lines of the division.

OPPOSITE ABOVE: As Illinois Central converted its freight operations to diesels in the 1950s, those parts of the system that were farthest from the coal fields of southern Illinois and western Kentucky were the first to receive the new locomotives. As a result, the Kentucky Division was one of the last bastions of IC's steam locomotives. As an NW2 shuffles cars at Louisville's Oak Street Yard, a 2-10-2 Central-type, #2814, departs with a southbound freight in March 1957. (Jack B. Fravert)

OPPOSITE BELOW: Production of EMD's GP9 ended in 1959 when it was replaced by the GP18. The IC took delivery of fifteen GP18s in March 1960 that allowed the retirement of IC's last steam locomotives. A second order was delivered in 1963, sporting low short hoods, a first for the IC. On September 23, 1967, examples of both versions were parked at the fuel pad at Oak Street Yard in Louisville, Kentucky. (Tom Smart, Dan Dover collection)

After Illinois Central acquired the CO&SW in 1896, the line became IC's Louisville and Memphis divisions, which were joined at Paducah. In 1911, the Louisville Division was renamed the Kentucky Division.

The CSX merger of 1980 and the creation of Norfolk Southern in 1982 led to a decline of interchange traffic that Illinois Central Gulf handled at Louisville. Unsuccessful in its bid to sell ICG or merge it with another railroad, IC Industries embarked on a program to downsize its railroad by selling off portions of it. On August 27, 1986 IC Industries sold the entire Kentucky Division to CG&T Industries. The new railroad was named the Paducah & Louisville Railway.

BELOW: Northbound train #104, the "Irvine S. Cobb," is minutes away from its 7:30 a.m. arrival at Central Station as it passes IC's Oak Street Yard in 1955. On the point of today's train is #2400, IC's first 4-8-2. Rolled out by the American Locomotive Company at Schenectady, New York, in October 1923, it was the first of thirty-five 4-8-2s that the IC would buy from ALCO while purchasing another twenty-five from Lima Locomotive Company. The new engines replaced 4-6-2s on IC's fastest passenger schedules and reigned supreme for three decades until they were replaced by diesels. Passenger service ended on the Kentucky Division on January 30, 1957, less than two years after this photo was taken. Number 2400 was dropped from the roster three years later, in February 1960. (Richard Baldwin)

OPPOSITE: The RoadRailer is an innovative cross between a truck trailer and a rail car. Developed by the Chesapeake & Ohio Railroad in the 1950s, the first examples were 29-feet long and were attached to the rear end of C&O passenger trains, carrying mail. Those hybrid trailers were out of service a few years later as passengers and mail contracts disappeared from the railroads in the 1960s.

The RoadRailer concept lay dormant until the 1970s when it was revived by Bi-Modal Corporation. The new RoadRailer was essentially a standard 45-foot highway trailer with a retractable set of rail wheels fastened to the tail. Several railroads operated test trains of the new RoadRailers in 1980 and 1981, but none committed. The numerous curves on the Kentucky Division restricted speeds on intermodal trains and Illinois Central Gulf had a tough time competing with trucks in the Louisville-Memphis market. So ICG decided to take a chance with the RoadRailers and inaugurated its "Supermode" service between Oak Street Yard in Louisville and Johnston Yard in Memphis in September 1981. The experiment lasted about a year with the final "Supermode" train operating on October 2, 1982. ICG replaced the RoadRailers with conventional intermodal equipment.

On a warm summer evening in July 1982, a yard tractor positioned an ICG RoadRailer on the ramp at Louisville's Oak Street Yard in preparation for the evening departure for Memphis. Once all of the trailers were set on the rails and connected, the adapter trailer was attached, and a locomotive backed onto the train. Tonight, Illinois Central Gulf GP11 #8728 will be in charge of the train to Memphis. (Two photos, Randy B. Olson)

The Louisville-Paducah Main Line

Illinois Central operated passenger service to Louisville through the 1950s. The last IC passenger schedules between Fulton and Louisville were trains #103 and #104, which were named the "Irvin S. Cobb" (Cobb was a Paducah-born journalist and humorist whose work appeared in the New York World and The Saturday Evening Post). The final runs of trains #103 and #104 came on January 30, 1957, ending scheduled passenger service on the Kentucky Division. But for years afterward, Illinois Central continued to run special trains to Louisville every May that brought the privileged to town to attend the Kentucky Derby.

In the 1960s, Illinois Central interchanged traffic with seven other Class One carriers at Louisville. To the north were the New York Central, Pennsylvania, Baltimore & Ohio and Chicago, Indianapolis & Louisville (popularly known as the Monon). To the south were the Louisville & Nashville Railroad and Southern Railway while the Chesapeake & Ohio Railroad came from the east. Illinois Central operations in Louisville were based at the railroad's Oak Street Yard, south of the city's commercial district.

With its numerous curves and grades, the main line between Louisville and Paducah was one of the IC's most challenging routes. The ancestry of the line was evidenced by its mile markers, which initiated at Louisville. After crossing the L&N's Louisville-Henderson main line (and Salt Creek) at West Point, the Louisville District began its climb out of the valley of the Ohio River, encountering Muldraugh Hill.

Two branch lines extended from the Louisville District. The Hodgenville District reached eastward from the main line at Cecilia. This district ran east 17 miles to Hodgenville. This town held the distinction of being the eastern-most station on the Illinois Central Railroad. The section between Elizabethtown and Hodgenville was abandoned in 1978. At Horse Branch, the Owensboro District ran northward almost 42 miles to Owensboro on the Ohio River. Illinois Central Gulf abandoned the entire district in 1981 and 1982.

BELOW: Diesels built for three different railroads were being serviced at Oak Street Yard engine facility on February 18, 1977. Parked between an ex-IC GP40 and a former GM&O GP30 was this set of SD9Rs that belonged to the Duluth, Missabe & Iron Range Railway. When the shipment of iron ore declined during the winter months, the DM&IR would often lease some of its surplus locomotives to other railroads on a short-term basis. (David E. Lichtenberg)

OPPOSITE ABOVE: IC's first order of GP18s disappeared into the sea of black GP7s and GP9s. But the engines from the second GP18 order, with their rakish low short hoods, stood apart from everything else on the property. The low noses on those units, such as #9424, leading this southbound freight at Louisville on September 5, 1966, would become standard on all subsequent IC locomotive orders. (Tom Smart, Dan Dover collection)

OPPOSITE BELOW: Twenty miles south of Louisville, at West Point, where the Salt River flows into the Ohio River, a three-span, through-truss bridge carried the Louisville District across the Salt. A southbound train exits the bridge on the morning of November 17, 1973. (Charles F. Buccola)

OPPOSITE ABOVE: Southbound ICG train LM-7 (Oak Street Yard in Louisville to Johnston Yard in Memphis) rolls across the Salt River bridge on an August evening in 1986. About a mile west of the bridge, the train will cross the L&N's Louisville-Henderson route and begin its ascent up Muldraugh Hill. (Mike Wild)

OPPOSITE BELOW: The southbound Cecelia Roadswitcher thunders over the trestle crossing Tioga Creek at Muldraugh, Kentucky, on the morning of July 15, 1982. This massive bridge was one of several on the Louisville-Paducah main line, therefore Kentucky Division employees in train crew service likely didn't have a fear of high places, or they wouldn't have lasted very long on the job. The Muldraugh bridge was built in the 1880's and was replaced with a concrete structure in 2012 by Illinois Central successor Paducah & Louisville. (Randy B. Olson)

ABOVE: IC's Hodgenville District split from the Louisville-Paducah main line at Cecelia to reach Hodgenville, the easternmost station on the railroad. Along the way, the district crossed the L&N's Louisville-Nashville main at Elizabethtown. On September 8, 1979, ICG GP10 #8021 climbs across the L&N with a short train. The interlocking was unmanned with the normal position for the L&N. It was the responsibility of ICG train crews to line the route across the busier railroad. (R. D. Acton, Jr.)

The yard at Central City was the crew change point where the Louisville and Paducah districts met. It also bordered the eastern edge of the West Kentucky bituminous coal field, which stretched from Beaver Dam to Dawson Springs and reached north to the Ohio River. In the early 1960s, 37 of the mines in this field were served by rail. The Illinois Central served 33 of them, 20 locally and 13 jointly with the Louisville & Nashville. The roundhouse at Central City serviced road power and switchers that worked the local coal mines and the yard was a marshalling point for coal trains destined for markets in the upper Midwest. The Louisville & Nashville Railroad's Owensboro & Nashville Subdivision passed beneath the Louisville District at Central City.

Between Central City and Dawson Springs, the Paducah District was operated as two parallel lines through the West Kentucky coal field. The southern line, which ran by way of

Greenville and Nortonville, was the original main line. The northern line, called the JK, was completed in 1924 and passed through Madisonville. This new line was built to provide additional access to coal mines located north of the original main line. The Louisville & Nashville's Evansville, Indiana-Nashville main line ducks under the JK just east of Madisonville Yard while the L&N line crossed the old CO&SW main at Nortonville.

While coal dominated the traffic profile of the Kentucky Division, two other commodities, chemicals and crushed stone, were also part of the mix. Several chemical plants located at Calvert City (east of Paducah) generated significant revenue for Illinois Central and Illinois Central Gulf. The IC also served a large quarry and a coal trans-loading facility at Grand Rivers.

The western end of the Paducah District crossed two tributaries of the Ohio River, the Cumberland and Tennessee Rivers. In

OPPOSITE ABOVE: The territory that the Louisville and Paducah Districts traversed between those namesake cities followed the Ohio River and crossed many of its tributaries along the way. Some of the IC's largest trestles were found on the Kentucky Division. While the bridges over the Salt Fork and Tioga Creek were both impressive structures, the title for the tallest and longest bridge on the division went to the trestle over Clifty Creek near the town of Big Clifty. This southbound train proceeded across the huge bridge on December 4, 1976, its engineer observing the 20 m.p.h. speed limit. (David E. Lichtenberg)

OPPOSITE BELOW: Leitchfield is a small community about 71 miles southwest of Louisville. The IC served several customers here and this large 24 x 100-foot wood depot was the town's freight and passenger station. It was also a train order office and a scheduled stop for passenger trains until the end of service on the Kentucky Division in 1957. Though looking a bit weatherbeaten, the station was still in service on Thanksgiving Day, November 25, 1982. A pair of GP10s and a caboose are parked on the house track with several company service cars. This depot would be sold to the Paducah & Louisville four years after this photo was taken, but was eventually demolished. (Scott D. Lindsey)

ABOVE: A northbound IC freight passes the Leitchfield depot on a bright September morning in 1970. The two lead locomotives are GP18s #9404 and #9407, part of a fifteen-unit order delivered to the IC in March 1960. That was the IC's first procurement of GP18s, and their arrival completed the dieselization of the railroad. In 1963 the IC bought another batch of fourteen GP18s, which were built with low noses. Numbers 9404 and 9407 were ten years old in this photo and had changed little during their life. Unlike so many GP7s and GP9s, only two of the IC's twenty-nine GP18s were rebuilt by Paducah. The rest were sold either to spin-off lines or other railroads or scrapped. (Lynn Moss)

the early 1940s, a dam was built across the Tennessee River at Jessup, requiring Illinois Central's line to be relocated. The new line carried the Paducah District across the top of the Kentucky Dam, which was completed in 1944. Construction of a second dam, this one across the Cumberland River, began in 1957. This project also included a 16-mile line relocation of the Paducah District. Illinois Central ran the first train over the new Barkley Dam on October 25, 1965.

ABOVE: When the fantrip chartered by the Louisville Chapter of the NRHS arrived at Central City, Kentucky, on October 27, 1957, Illinois Central 4-8-2 #2452 was cut away from the train and serviced while the train's riders toured the engine facilities. (Richard Baldwin)

BELOW: Two-thirds of Illinois Central Gulf's ALCO C-636 fleet lead a southbound train at Rockport in the summer of 1976. The Century 636 was ALCO's answer to EMD's 3600-horsepower SD45. The design enjoyed a reasonable degree of success on railroads that had experience operating other types of ALCO locomotives. But the six examples purchased by the IC in 1968 were truly anomalies on IC's mostly EMD roster. The big units spent most of their careers on the Kentucky Division, not far from the Paducah backshop where their various mechanical issues could be resolved. (Rick Grandish)

RIGHT: As #2452 was being serviced at Central City, the excursionists walked over to the round-house to photograph the engines that were on hand. Up front was one of the improved Central types, #2721, with a trio of 2-8-2s behind it. All the engines were in service. (Richard Baldwin)

BELOW: On a warm evening in August 1974, the crew of an empty hopper train and some clerks were engaged in a game of pitching washes — similar to pitching horseshoes, but using large washes that were pitched at a hole in the ground — in front of Illinois Central Gulf's Central City yard office. Central City was situated midway between Louisville and Paducah and this yard was once busy with coal traffic from mines in the western Kentucky coal fields. The ICG was still hauling a considerable amount of bituminous tonnage on the Kentucky Division at the time this scene was recorded but the flow of black diamonds had been ebbing for several years. Like southern Illinois coal, that from western Kentucky also contained higher amounts of sulfur, making it less desirable as environmental regulations for coal-burning power plants increased incrementally through the 1970 and 1980s. The decline in revenue from coal traffic was a factor in IC Industries' decision to sell the Kentucky Division to CG&T Industries in 1986. (J. Allen Hicks)

OPPOSITE ABOVE: Train LM-1 is stopped on the main in front of the depot at Ft. Knox on October 13, 1975. It's waiting for a northbound, possibly ML-4 or a unit coal train, to head into the siding. The head brakeman has walked up to line the switch for the siding so the northbound won't have to stop. After the train passes, he will line the switch back for the main and LM-1 will pick him up on the fly and leave in a cloud of ALCO smoke. (S. A. Lee, Dan Dover collection)

OPPOSITE BELOW: Southbound train LM-1 winds through a pair of curves at Fort Knox on December 4, 1976. This schedule forwarded freight from Oak Street Yard in Louisville to Johnston Yard at Memphis. With the acquisition of the Chesapeake, Ohio & Southwestern in 1896, Louisville became an important source of traffic for the IC. In addition to serving several large industries in the city, the IC interchanged with seven other railroads, which provided direct rail connections to the Great Lakes and the Atlantic seaboard. During the 1960s and 1970s, the railroads that IC connected with at Louisville merged to eventually form the two dominant carriers of the eastern U.S., Norfolk Southern and CSX. As a result, ICG's Louisville interchange traffic such as that handled on today's LM-1 continued to decline through the 1980s. (David E. Lichtenberg)

TWO-PAGE SPREAD: This southbound train is slowing as it prepares to stop at the Princeton yard in July 1974. Its crew will set out and pick up cars for the Evansville District, which branched off the Louisville-Paducah main line at Princeton. At one time, the Evansville and Paducah Districts crossed at Princeton's two-story brick passenger depot near the town's business district. The depot had stood just around the distant curve in the first of these two views taken from the Maple Street overpass. The station was demolished after the end of passenger service and the diamond was removed. Operations on the northern and southern legs of the Evansville District were based at Princeton's yard west of town, visible in the distance in the second view. There still appears to be quite a bit of activity at the yard, but the prospects for the Evansville District's survival would soon dim as the ICG sold and abandoned similar unprofitable branch lines across its system. (Both photos, Randy B. Olson)

OPPOSITE ABOVE: An empty Illinois Central Gulf aggregate train is dwarfed by mountains of limestone as it pulls onto the loading track at the quarry in Grand Rivers, Kentucky, in January 1981. The three SD40s on this train are painted in the ICG's final paint scheme, which appeared in June 1979. The new paint job was part of an effort to create a fresh image for ICG, which was still looking for a merger partner. Negotiations with Southern Railway had hit a dead end the previous year so IC Industries tried to put on a good face with the new scheme. In addition to many SD40s, all the SD20s, practically all the GP11s and most of the SW14s built by Paducah for ICG received this new image. This quarry sits between the Tennessee and Cumberland Rivers, just below Kentucky and Barkley Dams. (Charles F. Hinrichs)

OPPOSITE BELOW: In March 1982, an ICG roadswitcher with a couple of newly rebuilt SW14s passed another job that was working the Airco chemical plant at Calvert City, Kentucky. Rebuilt locomotives from the Paducah shop would often get a break-in run on one of these Calvert City turns. These chemical plants were built here in the late 1940s and early 1950s with ample electrical energy made available from Tennessee Valley Authority's nearby Kentucky Dam. Transportation was provided by the IC and barges on the Tennessee River. Like the industrial plants along Illinois Central's Baton Rouge District in Louisiana, the traffic generated at Calvert City was a solid revenue source for the railroad. (J. Allen Hicks)

ABOVE: Calvert City was named for Potilla Willis Calvert, who gave a portion of his land to an Illinois Central predecessor, the Elizabethtown & Paducah Railroad. He specified that a station be built near his home, which then served as a starting point for the town in 1871. The community was called Calvert until 1957 when the current name was adopted. The engineer on eastbound train ML-2 (Memphis-Louisville) opens up the throttle as the train pulls across the South Main Street crossing at Calvert City on November 11, 1980. The Paducah District was double track from Paducah to Gilbertsville Junction, about three miles east of where this photo was taken. (J. Allen Hicks)

BELOW: November 5, 1975, would have otherwise been a routine day for the crew working the ICG local south of Hopkinsville, Kentucky, but they all became celebrities when they were assigned the ICG's bicentennial unit, "The American Eagle." This GP38AC, formerly IC #9503, was repainted in this special scheme as ICG's tribute to America's 1976 bicentennial and was sent on tour across the Illinois Central Gulf system, including the Evansville District. Once the engine stopped on the former Tennessee Central bridge over U.S. Route 41 south of Hopkinsville, everyone in the cab came out to pose for the photographer. The special unit continued to roam the railroad through 1976, often on display to the public, to celebrate the nation's birthday. This was actually the ICG's second unit painted in this bicentennial scheme; it was preceded by GP38AC #9510 in early March 1975. Less than a week after that engine had been repainted, "The American Eagle" was assigned as lead unit on Chicago-New Orleans intermodal train #53. The train struck a tractor-trailer tank truck loaded with crude oil south of Brookhaven, Mississippi, resulting in the death of the engineer and the fireman sustaining serious injuries. The charred hulk was moved to the Paducah backshops as Woodcrest Shops, located near Chicago, proceeded to transform number 9503 into the new "American Eagle." A plaque, identical to that which was given to engineer Thomas F. Dickerson's widow, was mounted on the back wall of this replacement unit's cab. (Rick Grandish)

OPPOSITE ABOVE: In June 1978, a trio of Geeps works the TOFC ramp at Ashland City, Tennessee, on the former Tennessee Central. In less than two years, ICG would petition the Interstate Commerce Commission to abandon the entire line between Hopkinsville and Nashville. (J. Allen Hicks)

OPPOSITE BELOW: Of the railroads that served Nashville, the Illinois Central was a minor player, so TC's modest locomotive facility in the city was sufficient to fulfill IC/ICG's needs. On July 13, 1974, these two ICG engines were seen idling in the Music City. (David M. Johnston)

The Evansville District

At Princeton, the Evansville District joined the Paducah District. The Evansville District was, by far, the largest branch of the Kentucky Division. In terms of operations, the district was comprised of two separate lines, each extending from the Paducah District at Princeton. Into the mid-1960s, the northern section ran from Evansville, Indiana, crossed the Ohio River via trackage rights on the L&N bridge at Henderson, Kentucky, and wound its way through West Kentucky to Princeton. Mileposts on the district were measured from Evansville. Two branches extended from the northern section of the Evansville District. The Uniontown District went north from the Evansville District at Morganfield (mile 34) while the Providence District went east from Evansville District at Blackford at mile 62. The Uniontown District was abandoned in 1982 and four years later, the Princeton-Morganfield portion of the Evansville District was sold to Pyro Energy Company, which then operated the line as the Tradewater Railway.

The southern portion of the Evansville District extended southward from Princeton to Gracey then turned east and ran to Hopkinsville. The southern section of the Evansville District connected with three other railroads: the shortline Cadiz Railroad at Gracey, and the L&N and the Tennessee Central at Hopkinsville. The Tennessee Central was a regional road that ran from eastern Tennessee, through Nashville, to meet the IC at Hopkinsville. After the TC slipped into bankruptcy in 1968, its assets were purchased by the IC, Louisville & Nashville and Southern Railway.

Illinois Central acquired 76 miles of the TC from Hopkinsville, Kentucky, to Nashville, Tennessee on September 1, 1968. This purchase represented the final addition to the Illinois Central before the Gulf, Mobile & Ohio merger of 1972. Illinois Central Gulf operated the former TC to Nashville until 1981, when it was allowed to abandon from Fort Campbell to Ashland City. The Ashland City-Nashville segment was taken over by a new short line, the Nashville & Ashland City, in December 1981. The following year, to ensure rail access to Fort Campbell, the United States

ILLINOIS CENTRAL

OPPOSITE ABOVE: The Illinois Central's Paducah freight house, once busy handling less-than-carload, or LCL, freight for the city's shippers, stands silent on this April afternoon in 1978. The single ICG boxcar parked beside it may only be delivering company supplies. At the dawn of the 20th century, railroads held a virtual monopoly on LCL shipments. All this traffic would pass through freight houses such as Paducah's to horse-drawn wagons for local delivery. When motor trucks began to replace the horses, the railroads started to lose the LCL business. As roads between cities improved, shippers began to rely entirely on trucks. The IC, like other railroads, tried to get in on the action by offering its own LCL truck delivery service at key cities in the 1930s and 1940s. But, by the late 1960s, the railroad had lost all of this business to motor carriers. (J. Allen Hicks)

OPPOSITE BELOW: In July 1986, IC #1306 and booster #1300B shoved caboose #9445 toward ICG's North Yard as the brakeman protected the back-up move. The two locomotives are SW13s, which were rebuilt by Paducah shops incorporating a sealed carbody, centralized air intake systems and modular electrical systems. Paducah produced a dozen SW13s and three cabless booster versions between 1971 and 1975. (J. Allen Hicks)

ABOVE: Illinois Central 0-8-0 #3526 was working North Yard at Paducah in the mid-1950s, just below the bridge that connects the Paducah & Illinois Railroad with the IC's Paducah District. At the time this photo was taken, the IC had replaced many of its steam locomotives with diesels, but there were still a few places on the railroad where steam could be found working. Paducah was one of the last strongholds of IC steam. Illinois Central bought 70 of these 0-8-0s between 1921 and 1929. The first 55 came from Baldwin Locomotive Works while the final batch of 15 was built by Lima Locomotive Works. This particular engine was built for Illinois Central's second order of 0-8-0s from Baldwin, delivered in September 1922. It was retired in December 1959. (Richard Baldwin)

Army assumed operation of the ex-TC line from Fort Campbell to Hopkinsville, under the name Fort Campbell Railroad.

Due to lack of maintenance, the Princeton-Hopkinsville portion of the Evansville District deteriorated through the late 1970s and into the 1980s. The ICC granted ICG permission to abandon the line in 1984, but the Cadiz Railroad then purchased the track between Princeton and Gracey. The Cadiz operated the line for four more years until it went out of business in 1988.

Paducah - Capital of the Kentucky Division

The southern end of the Kentucky Division was anchored at Paducah, where the division's administrative and dispatching offices were situated. Like Louisville, Paducah was a community that was established by trade on the Ohio River. Traffic between the Kentucky Division and the rest of the IC system was handled through Paducah at a pair of end-to-end freight yards, North and South yards.

After entering the eastern side of the city, the Paducah District skirted downtown and crossed the Nashville, Chattanooga & St. Louis' Bruceton, Tennessee-Paducah branch. Just south of this crossing, the east end of the Paducah & Illinois Railroad connected with the NC&StL. The Paducah & Illinois Railroad was IC/ICG's connection to the Edgewood Cutoff. After NC&StL's successor, Louisville & Nashville, abandoned its line to Paducah in 1982, Illinois Central Gulf took over the short stretch of track to connect the Paducah District with the P&I Railroad.

A short distance west of the NC&StL crossing, the Paducah District turned southward and met the Mayfield District at North Yard. The eastern end of P&I trackage crossed over the Mayfield District where North and South yards joined. Beyond South Yard, the Mayfield District continued southward almost 44 miles to Fulton, Kentucky. After the Edgewood Cutoff was built, Kentucky Division traffic was routed over the Paducah & Illinois Railroad. By the early 1980s, few ICG trains were using the Mayfield District and the section between Fulton and Clayburn was abandoned in 1983.

BELOW: Another engine that was working at Paducah in the late 1950s was 2-10-0 #3619, seen here shoving a cut of hoppers at South Yard. This locomotive was part of a group of fifteen (the only Decapods that the IC owned) that the Paducah shops assembled using boilers from 2-8-2s and modified running gear from 2-10-2s. (Richard Baldwin)

OPPOSITE ABOVE: Four ICG C636s repose near Paducah's South Yard diesel house in August 1975. All six of the ALCOs would be struck from the roster four years later and traded to Precision National Corporation. The departure of the big Centuries brought an end to Illinois Central's long association with the American Locomotive Company and its predecessors. Like the IC, American Locomotive, also known as ALCO, was the product of mergers and acquisitions. In 1901, the Schenectady Locomotive Engine Manufactory merged with seven other locomotive builders to form the company, making it America's biggest locomotive company. The IC had purchased locomotives from several of these companies for decades prior to the consolidation. In 1905, the Rogers Locomotive Company of Paterson, New Jersey, was added to American Locomotive. The IC's first locomotives were built by Rogers in 1852. ALCO built many steam locomotives for the IC through the first quarter of the 20th century, but the Depression forced the railroad to curtail purchases of new engines. Illinois Central 4-8-2 #2459, delivered in November 1926, was the last steam locomotive built by ALCO for the IC. ALCO built eight 600-horsepower diesel switchers for the IC in 1935 to work Congress and South Water Street Yards and General Electric built a pair of massive transfer units in 1936 for IC's Chicago lakefront freight operations. After that, every diesel locomotive purchased by the IC until 1967 would be built by General Motors. ALCO stopped building locomotives in 1969, the year after the IC's C636s were delivered. (J. Allen Hicks)

OPPOSITE BELOW: A quartet of SD20s are tied onto an empty coal train at South Yard in Paducah on July 15, 1988. The crew's bags on the ground near the lead unit seem to indicate that the train has either just arrived at the yard or will be departing soon. (Greg C. Sieren)

BELOW: After the ICG sold the Kentucky Division to CG&T Industries, it maintained interchange with the new railroad with a local that ran from Fulton to Paducah and back. On August 13, 1994, Illinois Central train FPF, the Fulton-Paducah turn, departed Paducah & Louisville's North Yard and is seen passing South Yard Junction on Paducah & Illinois Railroad. The line to the right, seen in this view from the Old Mayfield Road overpass, is a connection to the north end of P&L's South Yard. The fourth locomotive in the train's engine consist is Kansas City Southern SD60 #741. It was repainted at VMV Industries, the company that took over the Paducah shops, and is on its way back to the KCS. (Kirk Reynolds)

OPPOSITE ABOVE: On June 10, 1988, an empty ICG coal train passes the east end of CR siding on the Paducah & Illinois Railroad. It's on its way to be loaded at a mine in southern Illinois and will continue on the P&I across the Ohio River to Metropolis Junction where it will get on the Bluford District. Centralized traffic control was installed on the P&I in 1929. It was one of the earliest CTC projects with the operator's office located at Metropolis Junction. The IC took over operational control of the P&I on Jan 1, 1930. The P&I dispatching duties were moved to IC's St. Louis Division offices at Carbondale, Illinois, in 1961 and then to Chicago in 1969. (Greg C. Sieren)

OPPOSITE BELOW: Northbound ICG train FPF (Fulton-Paducah Turn) pulls off the Edgewood Cutoff at Maxon and heads for Paducah Yard on August 3, 1987. The last locomotive in the consist is an industrial switcher that is going to VMV Locomotive in Paducah for repairs. (Greg C. Sieren)

On the western edge of Paducah, Illinois Central's East Cairo District split from the P&I at CR Junction and crossed the Edgewood Cutoff at Maxon, about five miles west of CR Junction. A connection track at Maxon facilitated the operation of Illinois Central (later, Illinois Central Gulf) trains on the Edgewood Cutoff between Fulton and Paducah by way of the East Cairo District. Beyond Maxon, the East Cairo District served a United States Department of Energy facility a few miles west of the Cutoff. As part of the Kentucky Division sale to P&L, Illinois Central Gulf included the East Cairo District in the transaction. Paducah & Louisville changed the name to the Maxon District. Canadian National trains continue to operate to Paducah over the Maxon District through a trackage rights agreement with the Paducah & Louisville.

OPPOSITE: The sale of ICG's Kentucky Division to CG&T Industries in August 1986 was a month away when the photographer captured this image of the front entrance of the division offices at Paducah. A sign on the right-side door states that applications for employment weren't being accepted at the time. (J. Allen Hicks)

BELOW: Pride among the employees of the Paducah shops is evident in the signs that were displayed above the building entrance on May 26, 1975. After the sale of the facility to VMV Enterprises, the sign was repainted into the paint scheme worn by VMV's lease fleet. (David M. Johnston)

Paducah Shops

At the beginning of the 20th century, the Illinois Central was made up of its charter lines in Illinois and a vast conglomeration of short lines and regional railroads it had bought or leased over the previous two decades. The hundreds of steam locomotives in the railroad's fleet were built by a variety of builders to a wide range of specifications and were maintained at numerous roundhouses scattered across the system. While the railroad was buying dozens of new locomotives every year, many of IC's older locomotives had seen better days. Possessing a fleet of both modern and older steam locomotives, Illinois Central needed to consolidate its heavy locomotive repair and rebuild work into one facility. Many existing locations were considered, but all were rejected for various reasons. As it would turn out, the name Paducah came to be synonymous with Illinois Central locomotives.

The administration of Charles Markham chose Paducah as the site for its new locomotive backshop in 1923 and construction of the

BELOW: It's June 1976 and the rebuilding program at Paducah is running full bore. In addition to rebuilding ICG's older power, the shop was also contracted to recondition units for several other customers. A pair of freshly rebuilt Geeps for the Rock Island have just been rolled out as ex-Detroit, Toledo & Ironton GP9 #984 awaits its transformation into ICG GP10 #8394. In line ahead of it is ALCO C-636 #1101, the only member of its class relettered ICG. (Randy B. Olson)

OPPOSITE ABOVE: This panoramic view of the main bay of the Paducah shop taken on March 27, 1975, reveals the range of work that the shop was handling that day. Two of the Illinois Central Gulf's C636s are on hand as well as a fellow alumnus of ALCO, a Louisville & Nashville C420. Another foreign visitor, a Norfolk & Western SD35, appears to have collision damage being repaired. Beyond it, ICG's final SW13, #1311, is taking shape. In the distance, parts for GP8s and GP10s are staged on the shop floor. (Bob Schmidt, Kirk Reynolds collection)

OPPOSITE BELOW: After it was involved in a wreck in late 1975, Illinois Central Gulf GP30 #2278 was taken to Paducah where it was given a new front end the following summer. This engine was built as GM&O #529 in September 1963, the next-to-the-last GP30 delivered to the railroad. This unit was returned to service after the wreck damage was repaired with no further improvements. In 1981, the Paducah shops would remanufacture two GP30s into the new GP26 model. The program, planned to convert the fleet of GP30s and GP35s into the new model, never proceeded past those first two engines, ICG #2601 and 2602. ICG #2278 was eventually remanufactured by VMV Industries into a road slug for CSX as its 2263. (Randy B. Olson)

facility was completed four years later. A decade after the shop opened, as the nation's economy began to emerge from the Depression, the IC initiated a comprehensive program to rebuild many of its locomotives. This program continued for several years and provided the railroad with a modern fleet of steam locomotives that not only enabled the IC to cope with the demands of wartime traffic levels, but also to postpone conversion of its freight operations to diesels until the late 1950s. The last steam locomotives to operate on the IC served on the Kentucky Division in early 1960.

With the retirement of steam power, the Paducah shop was retooled to perform heavy maintenance on diesel locomotives. In the mid-1960s, as many of the diesels that had replaced Illinois

Central's steam engines were themselves beginning to show their age, the railroad began another locomotive rebuilding program. Each locomotive was completely disassembled, and every component was completely rebuilt. The first rebuilt unit was completed in May 1967 and, over the course of the next 16 years, hundreds of diesels were rebuilt by the Paducah shop for Illinois Central, Illinois Central Gulf and several other railroads. The last locomotive to be rebuilt by the ICG at the Paducah backshop was completed at the end of 1982. When IC Industries sold the Kentucky Division to CG&T Industries in 1986, the Paducah shop was included in the transaction. VMV Enterprises took over the facility and resumed locomotive repair and rebuilding operations.

OPPOSITE ABOVE: Three new cabs are lined up in Paducah's main bay, ready to be placed on locomotive frames. The cab in the middle was a new design that Paducah began building in 1977. It was based upon the post-1963 standard EMD cab and was created to use on GP10s rebuilt from cabless GP9Bs acquired from the Union Pacific. There was such a demand for rebuilt locomotives from Paducah that most of the previous year's production went to railroads other than the ICG. The new angular cab would eventually be applied to all Paducah rebuilds during the final years of the ICG. (Randy B. Olson)

OPPOSITE BELOW: Their days of glamour long past, this long line of E-units was parked near the Paducah shop in March 1978. A few will be rebuilt for commuter service in New Jersey, but most would be scrapped. This view is looking south and, in the distance, a northbound ICG train can be seen beyond the Chester Hack Drive overpass in the center right of the photo departing North Yard. The track on which these locomotives were parked once led to IC's ferry slip at Paducah. Before the construction of the Metropolis bridge, IC operated a transfer boat between Paducah and Brookport, Illinois. The completion of the bridge ended the ferry service, but this line would continue to serve for local traffic and access to the new Paducah shops. All of the track switches on the right side of the photo lead into the various supply yards for the shop complex. (Steve H. Forrest)

ABOVE: A string of brand-new ICG GP11s, #8744, #8748-8750 and SD20s #2012-2014, are lined up outside the shop at Paducah on September 1, 1980. This batch of GP11s was the next-to-the-last of this model to be turned out by Paducah. Three more GP11s, #8751-8753, were completed before production of the model ended in 1981. Production of the SD20s would continue through 1982 and, with the delivery of ICG SD20 #2041, the last locomotive rebuilding program for the parent railroad would take place at the Paducah shops. (David M. Johnston)

The Cairo District — South End — and the Jackson District

Beyond Fulton, the Cairo District continued southward to Jackson, Tennessee, where it joined the Jackson District. Illinois Central's route to Birmingham, Alabama, also diverged from the Cairo District at Jackson. The largest community between Nashville and Memphis, Jackson was also the principal rail center between those cities.

The IC main line through Jackson saw its glory days in the 1890s, following the completion of the Ohio River bridge and before the acquisition of the Chesapeake, Ohio & Southwestern. After most passenger and freight traffic was rerouted through Memphis, the role of the former Mississippi Central faded to that of a secondary main line. Nonetheless, Illinois Central's presence in Jackson, Tennessee, would remain strong for years to come.

During the last decades of the 1800s and into the new century, economic growth in the southeastern states drew the attention of IC's directors. Development of the iron and steel industry in Birmingham's environs no doubt prompted their decision to begin construction of a line to the city in 1906. The new extension would head southeast from Jackson. But there was another reason for the Illinois Central to go to Birmingham.

In 1907, E. H. Harriman acquired control of the Central of Georgia Railway, a system that ran through the middle of Georgia

BELOW: Northbound Illinois Central Gulf train BC-4 crosses the Bluford District after arriving at Fulton, Kentucky, from Birmingham on May 26, 1988. The bulkhead flatcars loaded with pulpwood will be set out here and forwarded to the Westvaco Paper plant at Wickliffe, Kentucky, on the Fulton-Cairo Turn. In the foreground, an empty Chicago & North Western grain train is heading north on the Cairo District. A few weeks after this photo was taken, Norfolk Southern took control of the Cairo District south of Fulton. (Kirk Reynolds)

OPPOSITE ABOVE: This venerable wooden structure near Fulton's downtown served as the community's passenger depot for three quarters of a century. After Amtrak moved to a pre-fabricated structure north of town in 1979, the old station was torn down. (Frank E. Ardrey, Jr., David P. Oroszi collection)

OPPOSITE BELOW: On this April afternoon in 1971, southbound train #1, the *City of New Orleans*, eased into the Fulton depot for its scheduled ten-minute station stop. The next three photos on the following pages show more of this event. (J. Allen Hicks)

OPPOSITE ABOVE: A few passengers disembarked the "City" on this day. The porter assists them as they step off coach #2616. This car and the one ahead of it in this train, #2625, were built for the IC by Pullman Standard in 1947 as part of a 27-car order of streamlined lightweight coaches that were assigned to trains such as the "City of New Orleans" as well as those in the Chicago-St. Louis corridor and on the Iowa lines. (J. Allen Hicks)

OPPOSITE BELOW: The baggage handler hands up the last few parcels to the baggage car worker while the departing passengers board the train. In a few weeks, the operation of this schedule will be assumed by Amtrak. (J. Allen Hicks)

ABOVE: As the train pulls out of Fulton, a coach porter stands in the doorway of coach #2681, formerly heavyweight coach #2222 that was built in March 1918 amd modernized by IC's Burnham Shops. Like the baggage handlers on the platform, this porter and the car on which he's riding, face uncertain times. (J. Allen Hicks)

OPPOSITE ABOVE: On this afternoon in April 1968, the "City of New Orleans" prepares to depart Fulton for its namesake city. The bridge in the foreground carries the Cairo District over Harris Ford Creek. Just behind where the photographer stood, the northwest switch of the connecting track would convey this train, like all Chicago-Memphis passenger trains, toward the Mayfield District at Fulton Junction. (Morgan McIlwain)

OPPOSITE BELOW: After departing Fulton station, the "City's" observation car rounds the connecting track at Fulton Junction as the train heads for Oaks, where it will reach the Fulton District, the main line to Memphis. On the left edge of the photo, the telegraph line disappearing into the distance indicates the Cairo District's southern end heading for Jackson, Tennessee. The Mayfield District can be seen crossing in the background. (Morgan McIlwain)

ABOVE: The fuel and water on the northbound "City of Miami's" three E-units has been topped off at Fulton on this morning in January 1969 as the train is prepared to make its 10:00 a.m. departure. The 16-car train's length seems to indicate that patronage of the train was still relatively strong only a year and a half prior to the creation of Amtrak. (Phil Gosney)

and into eastern Alabama. The CofG's line to Birmingham gave the IC a connection to railroads that served Florida. Soon after its Birmingham line was completed, IC established operating agreements with the Central of Georgia and Atlantic Coast Line to create a through passenger route between Chicago and Florida.

In the early 1960s, the southern end of the Cairo District was an active piece of railroad, though not nearly as busy as the portion north of Fulton that handled a good portion of the Memphis traffic. Most of the trains that ran on the IC through Jackson, Tennessee, were going to or coming from Birmingham. By comparison, the Jackson District saw only local service.

South of Fulton, the Cairo District crossed two other railroads. The Nashville, Chattanooga & St. Louis' branch to Hickman, Kentucky, was intersected at Martin. After NC&StL

merged with the L&N in 1957, the branch through Martin remained in service until it was abandoned in the early 1980s. At Milan, Illinois Central shared a diamond and a passenger depot with Louisville & Nashville. This was L&N's Nashville-Memphis main line that still serves as CSX's route between those cities.

Entering Jackson from the north, the Cairo District crossed the Gulf, Mobile & Ohio's Mobile-St. Louis main line at Union Station. Built by the Mobile & Ohio, the depot served as a stop for the passenger trains of both the GM&O and the IC. The GM&O ended passenger service through Jackson in 1958, but Illinois Central passenger trains continued to make their stop at Union Station until July 1961, when IC moved its Jackson passenger stop to the freight house south of Sycamore Street. Illinois Central Gulf demolished the old M&O depot in 1975.

BELOW: A southbound Illinois Central Gulf train pulls into the siding at Milan, Tennessee, to perform its interchange work with the Louisville & Nashville on November 13, 1982. The L&N's Nashville-Memphis main line crossed the Cairo District at the distant depot, which was a joint facility serving both railroads. The Army Ammunition Plant at Milan provided both railroads with plenty of traffic during World War II, the Korean War and the Vietnam War, but ordnance production at the plant ceased in the first decade of the 21st century. (William C. Davis, David P. Oroszi collection)

OPPOSITE: On August 27, 1976, a southbound Illinois Central Gulf train with a former GM&O GP30 on the point held the siding at Martin, Tennessee, to meet another train. Leading the northbound was the ICG's only SD45, #7000, a former EMD demonstrator. The northbound was train #74, dispatch freight BC-4. The difference between the train number and the train symbol is that the number represents a specific schedule in the employee timetable while the symbol identifies a specific service to move traffic from a point of origin to a destination. In this case, BC-4 was a Birmingham to Chicago high-priority freight, or dispatch freight in IC parlance. (Both photos, Mike McBride)

In the 1950s, Jackson was home to IC's Mississippi Division headquarters, located in the railroad's office building between Chester and Sycamore streets, about a mile south of Union Station. A short distance south of the division offices was IC's freight house, which became IC's final passenger station in Jackson during the final years of its Chicago-Florida passenger service. Chester Street Yard was the first freight yard that IC used at Jackson before a larger facility, Frogmoor Yard, was built south of town. The roundhouse remained at Chester Street Yard, where steam locomotives were serviced until the Mississippi Division was dieselized in the mid-1950s. In the diesel era, the facility was used mostly for refueling. A short distance south of Chester Street Yard, the Cairo District passed over Nashville, Chattanooga & St. Louis' main line to Memphis on a short bridge.

The Cairo and Jackson districts and a connection track that led to the Birmingham line all converged at the south end of Frogmoor Yard, IC's main freight yard at Jackson. Through freights set out and picked up cars at Frogmoor for IC customers around town and along the Jackson District, as well as those that were interchanged with Jackson's two other railroads (GM&O and NC&StL). Illinois Central's route to Birmingham branched off from the Cairo District at J&SE Junction. Just south of the junction, where the Cairo and Jackson Districts met, the IC crossed GM&O's branch to Dyersburg, Tennessee, at Bemis.

The Jackson District ran just shy of 116 miles from Frogmoor Yard to Water Valley, Mississippi. While passenger service on the line ended just before World War II, seasonal strawberry specials that originated in Louisiana continued to run through Water Valley

and Jackson until after the war. By the late 1950s, business on the district had dwindled to a local freight that worked between Jackson and Water Valley. While the movement of traffic over the bustling Cairo District was protected by automatic block signals, the Jackson District was not equipped with block signals.

Two other railroads traversed the district. The Southern Railway's Memphis-Sheffield, Alabama, line crossed at Grand Junction, Tennessee. The Jackson District crossed the St. Louis-San Francisco (popularly known as the Frisco) at Holly Springs, Mississippi. Illinois Central maintained the interchange of freight traffic at both locations.

The Illinois Central's Jackson and Water Valley Districts met at Water Valley. Into the late 1920s, trains that ran between Jackson, Tennessee, and Canton, Mississippi, changed crews and engines at Water Valley. As larger locomotives went into service, engine districts were lengthened. The roundhouse at Water Valley was closed and the work that had been done there was moved to Jackson, Tennessee.

Fourteen miles south of Water Valley, the Mississippi & Skuna Valley Railroad connected with the Water Valley District at Bruce Junction. The 22-mile short line's primary customer was a lumber mill at its east end in Bruce, Mississippi.

BELOW: The lead engine on the northbound "City of Miami" is pulling across Sycamore Street as its train slows for the stop at Jackson, Tennessee, on July 13, 1968. Seven years earlier, the Illinois Central moved its Jackson passenger station from GM&O's Union Depot to the Chester Street freight house, seen in the upper left corner of this photo. In the upper right, all the stall doors at the Chester Street roundhouse were closed, but diesels were still serviced next to the sand tower and fuel rack. The former company supplies building next to the roundhouse appears to have been sold to a plywood company. Just out of the photograph to the left was the IC's Mississippi Division office building. It survives today, housing commercial offices, and is listed on the National Register of Historic Places, one of the few railroad buildings still standing in the city. Everything in this scene related to the railroad is now gone. (William I. White, Jack Ferry collection)

OPPOSITE: On an August morning in 1973, a pair of Illinois Central Gulf freights met at the Chester Street freight house in Jackson. In the first photo, a southbound train led by SD40A #6020 crosses Sycamore Street. This may be Chicago-Birmingham dispatch freight SE-1. The roadway overpass in the background is part of the U.S. Route 45 bypass around the city's business district and was the vantage point from which William White took his 1968 photograph, shown above. The photographer captured this sequence from the platform of Illinois Central's Chester Street passenger station, out of use since the "City of Miami" stopped running in 1971. Though it was no longer a passenger station when these photos were taken, ICG still used Chester Street as a train order office until all ICG traffic was moved to the ex-GM&O lines through town in the early 1980s. The northbound train, with SD40A #6008 on the point, is waiting in front of the office for clearance to proceed once the southbound passes. (James L. Jeffrey, Dan Dover collection)

BELOW: The southbound train shown passing Sycamore Street on the previous page has passed Frogmoor Yard and is now on the Jackson & South Eastern Railroad. The J&SE was a three-mile Illinois Central subsidiary that was built in 1907 as part of the IC's new route to Birmingham. It ran between the south end of Frogmoor Yard and Perry, on the Mobile & Ohio line to Corinth, Mississippi. The train is crossing the track of another GM&O predecessor, the Gulf, Mobile & Northern, at a crossing called Bemis. This GM&N line was a link between its main to Dyersburg, Tennessee, and the M&O's Iselin Yard. (James L. Jeffrey, Dan Dover collection)

OPPOSITE ABOVE: Although it was usually assigned to secondary passenger trains on the Iowa and Illinois Divisions, one of Illinois Central's GP9s equipped with a steam generator, #9219, found its way to Jackson in July 1968. It was parked at the Chester Street roundhouse, across the tracks from the freight/passenger station. IC's Chicago-Florida trains changed engines at Jackson, so Chester Street was a busy place during the steam era. (Morgan McIlwain)

OPPOSITE BELOW: Rather than expand its yard at Sycamore Street to handle the expected increase in traffic from its new route to Birmingham, the Illinois Central built a new facility, Frogmoor Yard, about a mile south of town in the first decade of the 20th century. When it was photographed on October 20, 1979, the old yard office at Frogmoor was showing its age. Some repairs had been made to the south end of the building, but the office was nearing the end of its career. The two photos on the following page, taken a decade earlier, attest to the building's advanced state of deterioration. (Richard Baldwin)

BOTH PHOTOS OPPOSITE: A southbound led by SD40A #6017 waits in front of the Frogmoor Yard office in October 1969 as a northbound train pulls off the connection track at J&SE Junction into the siding. In the distance, the train's cars are rolling through the junction where the J&SE and the Cairo and Jackson Districts all met. A new connection was built north of Jackson soon after the ICG merger and the Birmingham traffic was shifted to the old GM&O line through the city. By the early 1980s, the ICG had consolidated its Jackson operations at the ex-GM&O Iselin Yard and the facilities at Frogmoor and Chester Street were closed. (Bob McCord, John Fuller collection)

BELOW: When this photo was taken in August 1973, the thick line of bushes growing between the tracks and the Mississippi Central depot at Holly Springs, Mississippi, was evidence that this elegant building hadn't served as a passenger station for decades. The Illinois Central sold the station in 1942 to an individual who used it as a residence and business. It is still owned and maintained by the family. What we see here is in fact an 1886 addition by the IC that surrounded the original two-story brick MC station built in the 1850s; that building was incorporated into the new structure. The extensive renovation of this depot was one of the many improvements made to the Mississippi Central after Illinois Central took control. When the Chicago-New Orleans main line moved to Memphis in the late 1890s, this station soon became redundant. But, somehow, it has managed to survive for another 120 years. (Frank E. Ardrey, Jr., David P. Oroszi collection)

Until the late 1940s, the southern end of the Water Valley District joined the Grenada District at Memphis Junction, about a mile north of the depot at Grenada. As the Army Corps of Engineers built Grenada Dam across the Yalobusha River to create Grenada Lake, the Water Valley District south of Bruce Junction was relocated. The new connection, called W.V. Junction, was 5.5 miles north of Grenada.

The Water Valley District was merged into the Jackson and Grenada Districts on April 30, 1967. The line north of WV Junction became part of the Jackson District and the track south of WV Junction was absorbed by the Grenada District.

The Birmingham Route

Illinois Central's line to Birmingham was an amalgamation of 86 miles of IC track and trackage rights over three other railroads. The first leg of the route ran on the Mobile & Ohio (which later became the Gulf, Mobile & Ohio) from Jackson to Ruslor Junction, near Corinth, Mississippi. The three-mile long Jackson & South Eastern Railroad (an IC subsidiary) was built to bridge the gap between the Cairo District and the M&O on the south side of Jackson. The J&SE joined the M&O main line at Perry, a couple of miles south of M&O's Iselin Yard. Illinois Central trains travelled 51 miles over the Gulf, Mobile & Ohio from Perry to Ruslor Junction to reach the north end of IC's Birmingham District.

The Birmingham District was a single-track line that stretched about 80 miles across the northeastern corner of Mississippi and into the hills of northwestern Alabama. The route's scenic highlight was the towering trestle (Illinois Central's tallest) that carried the line high above Brush Creek near Hackleburg, Alabama. The district met only two other railroads, both at Corinth, Mississippi. The Corinth & Counce Railroad, a short line that served several industries near Corinth and others northeast of the city, connected with the IC at Corinth. Less than a mile down the line, the Birmingham District passed over Southern Railway's Memphis-Sheffield, Alabama route.

The southern end of the Birmingham District joined the Southern Railway's Sheffield, Alabama-Birmingham route at Haleyville, Alabama, where IC trains switched from home rails to those of Southern. They travelled 40 miles over the Southern to Jasper, where they would get on the Frisco's Memphis-Birmingham line (the Birmingham Subdivision) that would take them another 42 miles into Birmingham. Though this territory was not a "mountain" railroad when compared to western roads such as the Denver & Rio Grande Western, the undulating terrain south of Haleyville certainly kept engine crews on their toes.

Entering the city from the northwest, the passenger and freight trains that ran on the SLSF's Birmingham Sub parted ways at Thomas Junction. The freights proceeded through the junction,

BELOW: About a mile north of Corinth, Mississippi, IC's Birmingham District met the GM&O's Okolona District at Ruslor Junction. This junction once witnessed the passings of such colorful trains as IC's "City of Miami" and GM&O's "Gulf Coast Rebel." In September 1978, the power on northbound ICG train BC4 has left the train on the ex-IC main (to the right) and pulled north of the junction to pick up GP38-2 #9612 on the former GM&O main, where the photographer was standing. The engine consist is backing onto the Birmingham District to run down the siding to pick up the Corinth block of cars. The former GM&O train order office at this junction was closed when this photo was taken. (Tom C. Thornhill)

OPPOSITE ABOVE: Once BC4 completed its pick up at Ruslor Junction, the train continued northward to Jackson. The design of the train's caboose, ICG #199508, incorporated a new approach to a uniquely IC operating practice. For decades, IC cabooses featured a door on both sides that allowed crew members to safely catch train orders. In 1966, IC's Centralia car shop produced fifty examples of a new design of caboose that eliminated the side door, replacing it with an extended deck on each end. Crew members would be able to catch train orders while standing behind a side panel on the deck. The redesign also featured an extended-vision cupola. The caboose in this photo was part of IC's second order of the new-style cars, built by the Darby Corporation in 1968 as IC #9508. (Tom C. Thornhill)

OPPOSITE BELOW: The southbound Jackson-Corinth Turn has just arrived at Corinth, Mississippi, on January 11, 1986, and is heading for the interchange with the Corinth & Counce Railroad. When it finishes its work there it will shove back north, stopping to work the GMSR interchange at Ruslor Junction. (Scott D. Lindsey)

crossing the Birmingham Southern Railroad (a local terminal road that served the steel industry) and entered East Thomas Yard, a joint facility shared by Illinois Central, Frisco and Central of Georgia. East Thomas Yard was, in fact, a pair of parallel yards that were separated by the Frisco main line. The IC and CofG occupied the yard on the north side and the Frisco yard was on the south side. Central of Georgia trains stopped using East Thomas Yard after the CofG merged with the Southern in 1963 and CofG's trains were routed to Southern's Norris Yard.

Illinois Central and Frisco passenger trains took the connection at Thomas Junction to Frisco's Birmingham Belt Railroad and headed toward the city. They continued through Freight Yard Junction to 10th Avenue Tower then turned southeast and rolled into Terminal Station. As the "Seminole" and "City of Miami" made their station stop at Birmingham, Illinois Central and Central of Georgia crews traded places as the diesels were refueled and the water for their steam generators was topped off.

Built in 1909, Terminal Station served all of the railroads that offered passenger train service to Birmingham (with the exception

of the Louisville & Nashville, which maintained its own depot). Illinois Central shared ownership of the facility (which was operated by its parent company, the Birmingham Terminal Company) with Alabama Great Southern Railroad, Central of Georgia Railway, St. Louis-San Francisco Railroad, Seaboard Air Line Railroad and Southern Railway.

Through the 1960s, passenger train service on the railroads that served Birmingham faded. On June 3, 1969, the "Seminole's" schedule was truncated to a Chicago-Carbondale, Illinois, run, leaving the "City of Miami" as one of the few passenger trains still using Terminal Station. With so few passengers using the once-grand structure, Terminal Station was replaced with a smaller building. Demolition of the old station began in September 1969 and was completed in March 1970. More than six decades of Illinois Central passenger service ended when Amtrak took over its operations on May 1, 1971. The last Illinois Central passenger train to call on Birmingham, Alabama, was the northbound "City of Miami," making its final station stop in the city on the night of April 30, 1971.

BELOW: Northbound BC-4 waits at Haleyville, Alabama, for the new crew that will take it to Fulton on the evening of May 6, 1988. The lead unit, SD40 #6034, was originally GM&O #920 and was involved in a wreck. When it was repaired at Paducah, it received a new nose that was fashioned from one recovered from an old Geep. (Scott D. Lindsey)

OPPOSITE ABOVE: Three SD40s are in charge of a southbound ICG train on Southern Railway tracks at Lynn, Alabama, on February 19, 1976. The IC ran over the Southern between Haleyville and Jasper, Alabama, on its way to Birmingham. (Dennis E. Conniff, N. J. Molo collection)

OPPOSITE BELOW: Working Birmingham's Thomas Yard on July 5, 1980, this pair of GP8s carried eleven years' worth of grime and soot that had accumulated since being rebuilt at Paducah. (David P. Oroszi)

Changes after the Merger

After the ICG merger, the former Illinois Central and Gulf, Mobile & Ohio properties in Jackson were combined. The Cairo District became part of the St. Louis Division while the Jackson District went into the new Delta Division. The Birmingham District was incorporated into the new Alabama Division, which was largely made up of GM&O lines. A new connection was built between the Cairo District and the ex-GM&O Union City District at Conalco, a couple of miles north of where the two lines crossed at the M&O depot. The Chicago-Birmingham trains were then rerouted through town on the old GM&O and Frogmoor Yard was gradually shut down.

By the early 1980s, the days when the Jackson District was a busy main line were, but a distant memory and Illinois Central Gulf petitioned the Interstate Commerce Commission to abandon the line between Bemis and Coffeyville, Mississippi. Permission was granted. But before the tracks were pulled up, the Lafayette, Marshall & Benton Regional Authority purchased the line from Grand Junction, Tennessee, to Oxford, Mississippi, in March 1982. Natchez Trace Railroad (a subsidiary of Kyle Railways, Inc.) provided service to customers along the former Jackson District for about 10 years until another shortline operator, Pioneer Railcorp, took over in April 1992. As a wholly-owned subsidiary of Pioneer, the railroad reclaimed its heritage when it was renamed Mississippi Central Railroad Company in January 1993.

The remaining 11 miles of track at the southern end of the Jackson District (between W.V. Junction and Bruce Junction) was renamed the Waterloo Railway in 1985. The Waterloo was the surviving corporate entity of a former interurban line in Iowa that

BELOW: An engine consist of various models of ICG Paducah Geeps is prepared for its next trip northward at the East Thomas Yard engine house at Birmingham on May 14, 1978. (Donald A. Woodworth. Jr.)

OPPOSITE ABOVE: When compared to the flashier SLSF SW1500s that worked the Frisco's half of East Thomas Yard in the 1970s, IC SW7 #1204 looks a bit dowdy. It received a complete makeover in 1980 when it was rebuilt into ICG SW14 #1439 at Paducah. (Dennis E. Conniff)

OPPOSITE BELOW: An Illinois Central freight is prepared to begin its northward journey at Thomas Yard in 1971. Leading the train are two of IC's distinctive SD40A diesels. The frames of these engines were five feet longer than standard SD40s to accommodate 5000-gallon fuel tanks. While these units were assigned to IC's busiest main lines, they were especially well-suited to contend with the rugged profile of the railroad's Birmingham route. (Dennis E. Conniff, N.J. Molo collection)

OPPOSITE ABOVE: Southbound IC train #9, the "Seminole," was allotted a half-hour for its stop at Birmingham for refueling and a windshield wash. When the "Seminole" arrived on the morning of July 23, 1968, Central of Georgia E8s #812 and 811 were in charge. The CofG was an integral component of IC's Chicago-Florida passenger route from the beginning and these two units were the CofG's contribution to the "Seminole's" motive power pool in the diesel era. They were repainted to IC colors in 1959, though the nose logo was modified to identify the unit's true owner. (Phillip Kotheimer)

OPPOSITE BELOW: Central of Georgia E8s #811 and 812, wearing the IC's modified passenger paint scheme of the late 1960s, brought the southbound "Seminole" into Birmingham's Terminal Station on December 16, 1968. The station was opened in 1909, when the IC was completing its route into the city. It served for just 60 years and was demolished less than a year after this photo was taken. (Phillip Kotheimer)

ABOVE: When the southbound "Seminole" stopped at Terminal Station on this morning in December 1968, the train and the station were both nearing the ends of their lives. The following summer, the "Seminole" would become the Chicago-Carbondale "Shawnee," never to call at Birmingham again. During that same summer, a new and much smaller passenger station would replace Terminal Station and, by year's end, demolition of the grand structure would begin. (Mike R. Schafer)

Illinois Central and Rock Island had jointly owned since 1956. Rock Island sold its half to IC in 1968. ICG included what was left of the subsidiary Waterloo Railroad as part of the sale of the Iowa Division to Chicago, Central & Pacific in 1985. The "new" Waterloo was created to act as owner of several hundred freight cars owned on behalf of ICG.

Illinois Central Gulf's withdrawal from Jackson and Birmingham was completed in June 1988 when it sold the Cairo District south of Fulton, the Okolona District (the old M&O main line) between Jackson and Corinth, Mississippi, and the Birmingham District to Norfolk Southern. Intended as a shorter route for its traffic between St. Louis and Sheffield, Alabama, NS also arranged trackage rights for its trains over the Illinois Central

Gulf between Fulton and Centralia, Illinois. Norfolk Southern scheduled four manifest freights a day through Jackson as well as occasional extra trains.

But the new route did not work as well as Norfolk Southern's operating department had hoped and the St. Louis-Sheffield traffic stopped running through Jackson in July 1995. The former IC and GM&O trackage between Fulton and Corinth was leased to West Tennessee Railroad, which took over service to on-line customers on August 1, 2001. The Mississippi-Alabama Railroad Authority purchased what had been IC's Birmingham District from Corinth to Red Bay, Alabama, in 1995 and service over the line was provided by Redmont Railway. The rest of the district between Red Bay and Haleyville, Alabama, was abandoned.

ABOVE: On May 5, 1990, southbound Illinois Central intermodal train I01 passes the construction site of the Memphis Pyramid, which was originally built as a sports arena but now houses a shopping complex for a national retailer of outdoor recreational merchandise. By the late 1990s, Illinois Central had rerouted all of its freight traffic to the belt line around the city and the only trains to use the line through Central Station on a daily basis were Amtrak trains #58 and #59, the "City of New Orleans." (David M. Johnston)

OPPOSITE ABOVE: A road switcher, a yard engine and a shiny Volkswagen Beetle are parked next to the well-landscaped yard office at North Yard, a few miles north of downtown Memphis on June 9, 1974. (David M. Johnston)

OPPOSITE BELOW: A small engine facility at North Yard provided a place to service the switchers that worked the yard and local industries. In January 1974 NW2 #1007, SW7 #401 and GP7 #8963 were positioned around the sand tower awaiting their next assignment. (Steve H. Forrest)

Illinois Central's main line reached more than 900 miles from the shore of Lake Michigan at Chicago to the busiest port on the Gulf, New Orleans. The operational center of the railroad was positioned between those two cities at Memphis, Tennessee. An article that appeared in a 1962 issue of the Illinois Central's employee magazine described the Memphis Terminal as the railroad's "busy halfway point."

Though Fulton was actually closer to being an equal distance from Chicago and New Orleans, the epithet was certainly no exaggeration. Chicago was the only terminal that was home to more

Illinois Central employees than Memphis. A dozen Illinois Central passenger trains ran into, out of and through the city every day. All of the 25 dispatch freight schedules that passed through Memphis were reclassified at the terminal's main freight facility, Johnston Yard. On most days, as many as 80 Illinois Central switch engines were kept busy as they worked the various yards and local industries around town.

In the 1950s, Illinois Central interchanged freight with the seven other Class 1 railroads that served Memphis. Three came from the east: the Louisville & Nashville, the Nashville,

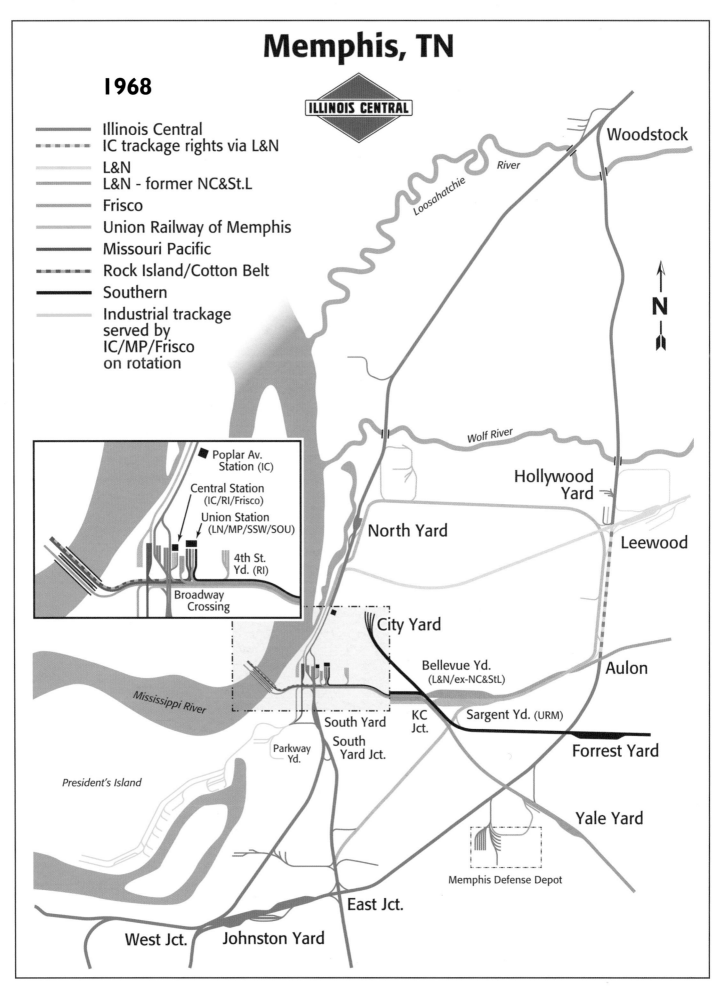

Memphis, TN

1968

ILLINOIS CENTRAL

Illinois Central
IC trackage rights via L&N
L&N
L&N - former NC&St.L
Frisco
Union Railway of Memphis
Missouri Pacific
Rock Island/Cotton Belt
Southern
Industrial trackage
served by
IC/MP/Frisco
on rotation

N

Loosahatchie River

Wolf River

Woodstock

Hollywood
Yard

Leewood

North Yard

Aulon

Poplar Av.
Station (IC)

Central Station
(IC/RI/Frisco)

Union Station
(LN/MP/SSW/SOU)

4th St.
Yd. (RI)

Broadway
Crossing

City Yard

Bellevue Yd.
(L&N/ex-NC&StL)

Sargent Yd. (URM)

KC
Jct.

Forrest Yard

Mississippi River

South Yard

Parkway
Yd.

South
Yard Jct.

Yale Yard

President's Island

Memphis Defense Depot

East Jct.

West Jct.

Johnston Yard

BELOW: A northbound ICG transfer rolls past one of the many industries located along the passenger main north of downtown as it heads for North Yard on June 9, 1974. (David M. Johnston)

BOTTOM: The southbound "City of New Orleans" climbs Beale Street Hill as it approaches Central Station on the evening of October 20, 1968. This photo clearly shows how steep the grade is, prompting the IC to build an alternate route around the city in the first decade of the 20th century. The track that the train is on is now part of the Memphis Area Transit Authority's Riverfront streetcar line while the other track is Canadian National's Memphis Subdivision. (William I. White, Steve H. Forrest collection)

BELOW: It's 11:15 on a late winter morning in 1969 and the "Mid-American" has just departed Central Station. This view looks northwest from an upper floor office in Central Station and shows train #4 negotiating the curves north of the station, the sharpest on the entire Chicago-New Orleans main line. On the horizon, construction of the Hernando de Soto Bridge across the Mississippi River has started as two concrete piers rise from the water. (Terry Foshee)

OPPOSITE ABOVE: The northbound "City of New Orleans" makes its departure from Memphis on a September afternoon in 1968. Illinois Central always put the interests of its customers first so when business car #9 and a second mail storage car were added to the train's consist at Memphis, they were attached behind the engines. This ensured an unobstructed view for the patrons riding in the train's observation car. (Phil Gosney)

OPPOSITE BELOW: On a pleasant evening in May 1969, southbound IC train #1, the "City of New Orleans," pulls into Central Station. This train was scheduled to arrive at Memphis' Central Station at 5:15 pm for a 15-minute station stop. By the time it arrived at Memphis it had covered 527 miles, well over half the distance to its destination of New Orleans. (Phil Gosney)

OPPOSITE: A coach porter stands ready to assist passengers as they board the "Mid-American" at Memphis in November 1968. Once the train is on its way, the porter will change into a white uniform jacket that will make him more visible to passengers. Upon arrival in Chicago, he will change back into his blue uniform jacket. The porthole window on the car behind the porter identifies it as one of six coaches that IC acquired from Missouri Pacific and modified into combination food-bar coaches. These were ¾ coach seating with a snack bar at the rear of the car. Operated by a single attendant with an offering of sandwiches, drinks and light snack items, this was the only food service on the "Mid-American." (Phil Gosney)

BELOW: The baggage handlers are still loading the baggage car as train #4, the "Mid-American," prepares to commence its northward journey to Chicago in September 1968. The round-top structure in the middle of the platform is a baggage elevator. (Phil Gosney)

Chattanooga & St. Louis and Southern Railway (Gulf, Mobile & Ohio trains used trackage rights to Memphis over the Southern from Corinth, Mississippi). Three lines came from the west: the St. Louis Southwestern (Cotton Belt), Missouri Pacific, and Rock Island. The seventh carrier, St. Louis San Francisco (Frisco) was the only railroad besides the IC to operate a route through Memphis—its Kansas City, Missouri–Birmingham main line. In addition to these trunk lines, the city was also served by the Union Railway of Memphis, a terminal switching road that was a subsidiary of Missouri Pacific.

Between the north end of the Memphis Terminal at Woodstock and East Junction at the south end, Illinois Central's traffic travelled over two routes. Passenger trains took the former Chesapeake, Ohio & Southwestern line that followed the Mississippi River and passed through IC's Central Station while most through freight schedules operated over a belt line that skirted the eastern side of the city. Prior to the IC/GM&O merger, both of these lines comprised the Memphis Terminal District.

The Passenger Main Line

Illinois Central's passenger main line through Memphis ran south from Woodstock, crossing the flood plain between the Loosahatchie and Wolf rivers. This single-track line was almost nine miles in length and was protected by automatic block signals.

The settlement that grew into the city of Memphis was established on the bluffs that overlook the Mississippi River. The builders of the Memphis & Paducah Railroad (a predecessor of Huntington's CO&SW) chose to locate its line below the bluffs, possibly to access the riverboat landings or perhaps because they could not obtain a right-of-way atop the bluffs through the city.

As Illinois Central put together its route through Memphis in the 1890s, it inherited two passenger depots from the previous owners. Poplar Avenue Station was located along the riverfront, near the city's business district, while Calhoun Street Station (also known as Union Depot) was located a couple of miles farther south. Both facilities were used by both IC trains and those of its

BELOW: Central Station was 60 years old when this photo was taken in November 1974. The building is certainly showing its age here, but will be fully refurbished a quarter century hence. This view is looking north on South Main St. (David M. Johnston)

OPPOSITE ABOVE: During its ten-minute station stop at Memphis, a working Railway Post Office car was added to the first out position on train #2, the "City of New Orleans". The train's engines would uncouple and pull north to allow a switch engine to add the car to the train. On November 24, 1968, the "City's" engine consist waits as the RPO is put on the train. (William I. White, Dan Dover collection)

OPPOSITE BELOW: Once the Post Office car was on the train and the switch engine had pulled out of the way, the "City's" engines coupled back onto the train and servicing was completed. Among the tasks performed by Central Station's staff was a quick wash of the lead unit's windshields. This photo was taken in June 1969 so it's certain that there's a pretty good coating of Mississippi bug debris on the glass. (Phil Gosney)

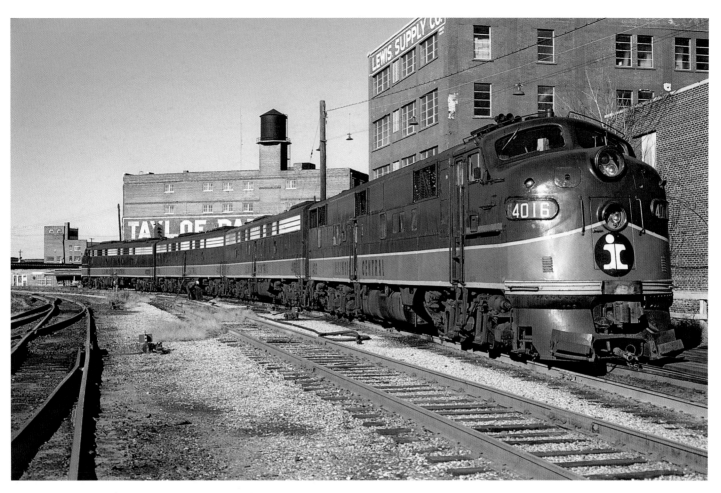

subsidiary Yazoo & Mississippi Valley. Shortly after the turn of the century, the Nashville, Chattanooga & St. Louis, Louisville & Nashville, and two lines that became part of the Frisco (the Kansas City, Memphis & Birmingham and the Kansas City, Fort Scott & Memphis) were also using Calhoun Street Station.

At the time, the railroads that served Memphis were working to establish a single passenger station that would accommodate all of them. They were unable to formulate a plan on which everyone could agree so five of the lines, NC&StL, L&N, Southern, St. Louis, Iron Mountain & Southern (which became part of the Missouri Pacific) and Cotton Belt, established their own joint passenger terminal, Memphis Union Station. The new station commenced operation in April 1912. In the meantime, Illinois Central moved forward with plans for a new passenger station of its own.

As Memphis's new Union Station was opened for business, construction of the facility that would replace IC's Calhoun Street Station got underway. The tracks were moved to the east and elevated above the streets, requiring southbound IC trains to climb a steep grade from the riverfront and turn through a sharp S-curve to reach the new station. Patrons of the Illinois Central, Yazoo &

Mississippi Valley, Frisco and Rock Island were accommodated in a temporary station as the old depot was demolished to make room for the new terminal.

Rising above the southwest corner of South Main Street and Calhoun Street, Grand Central Station opened in October 1914. It became Illinois Central's second busiest passenger facility, handling IC's Chicago-New Orleans trains as well as those of its subordinate Y&MV, the Frisco's traffic through Memphis and Rock Island's passenger trains. The office space that towered above the tracks served as home to the administrative offices of IC's Memphis Terminal and Memphis and Tennessee divisions.

The 1940s brought not only the surge of wartime traffic to Grand Central Station, but also a touch of elegance as the "Panama Limited," flagship of the railroad's Chicago-New Orleans service, was rejuvenated with diesel-powered streamlined trainsets. More new diesels and lightweight cars were delivered after the war to upgrade IC's passenger fleet, but, by the end of the decade, passenger service on the nation's railroads was beginning its long decline. As if to portend the future, the "Grand" was dropped from station's name in 1944.

BELOW: The northbound "City of New Orleans" clatters across the diamonds at Broadway as it pulls into Central Station in December 1969. Carrying the markers is dome coach #2210, which Illinois Central acquired from Missouri Pacific in 1967. (David M. Johnston)

OPPOSITE ABOVE: An IC SW7 drags a long cut of cars out of South Yard and as it pulls across the Frisco and MoPac tracks at Broadway on July 5, 1972. (Theo Sommerkamp)

OPPOSITE BELOW: In the mid-1980s, as IC Industries trimmed the Illinois Central Gulf down to a core Chicago-New Orleans system, a new image for the transformed railroad was developed. The new image was, for the most part, a reincarnation of IC's pre-1966 paint scheme for its freight locomotives. A modified version of this paint scheme with different lettering and a new logo would adorn the locomotives of the "new" Illinois Central Railroad after it was spun off by Whitman Corporation, the successor to IC Industries. On November 1, 1987, GP40 #3100 and GP38-2 #9619 pull a southbound inspection train through Memphis. Norfolk Southern theatre car "Buena Vista" was borrowed for the tour. (David M. Johnston)

Just as the magnificent era of steamboat travel on the Mississippi came to an end in the 1860s, it seemed that the nation's passenger trains were also heading for extinction a century later. Though Illinois Central's passenger service through Memphis remained august into the mid-1960s (even as the city's other railroads were trying to curtail theirs), IC's new president, William B. Johnson, did not share his predecessor's enthusiasm for this service. As a result, a number of IC passenger schedules serving Memphis were rearranged in March 1967. Rock Island stopped providing passenger service to Memphis on November 10, 1967, and Frisco's last passenger train passed through town about a month later on December 9.

The 1970s was a decade that saw Central Station decline into an empty edifice. When Amtrak took over passenger services on most of the nation's railroads on May 1, 1971, Memphis was left with a single passenger train/route running through town, the "City of New Orleans. After the Illinois Central Gulf merger, the company offices in Central Station were vacated as IC Industries moved the work performed there to other locations. By the mid-

1980s, the building was almost completely empty, the only tenant being Amtrak.

Central Station was saved in the 1990s by a development project hosted by private investment and the City of Memphis. The upper floors of the structure are now occupied by up-scale residences. Illinois Central routed the last freight schedules using the passenger route along the city's riverfront to the belt line on the east of side of town, leaving Amtrak's "City of New Orleans" as the only train operating through Central Station.

Streetcar service in Memphis was discontinued in June 1947, but the Memphis Area Transit Authority restored trolley service to the city's business district in the spring of 1993. The initial route runs 2.5 miles down Main Street and ends at Central Station. The second route, the Riverfront Line, went into operation in 1997 and parallels the Main Street route. The Riverfront Line shares much of its right-of-way with the former IC passenger route along the riverfront until it turns eastward and connects with the southern end of the Main Street line in front of Central Station.

BELOW: In this view looking west on the Frisco and Mopac mains, track workers tighten the bolts on a joint bar as an IC switcher pulls northward at Broadway on April 28, 1973. On the other side of the crossing, a small shed protects the white sedan that belonged to the switch tender who operated the switches at the south end of Central Station. In the upper center of the photo, the small white building is the operator's office at Kentucky Street. On the horizon in the distance are the Frisco and Harahan Bridges across the Mississippi River. (Steve H. Forrest)

OPPOSITE ABOVE: The roundhouse at South Yard was shut down when Illinois Central stopped using steam locomotives through Memphis, but diesel passenger units were serviced at one of the remaining shop buildings until it was also closed in 1969. (Terry Foshee)

OPPOSITE BELOW: By the late 1960s, passenger services on most American railroads were in a state of severe neglect, but the Illinois Central remained a class act. On October 19, 1967, a worker at the South Yard diesel shop washes a pair of freshly-painted E8s. (William I. White, Steve H. Forrest collection)

OPPOSITE ABOVE: During the mid-1970s, Illinois Central Gulf ran four piggyback schedules between Chicago and New Orleans. All of these trains were routed through downtown Memphis on the passenger main. On an afternoon in March 1977, a southbound piggyback train rolls under the McLemore Avenue viaduct as a switcher works the yard. (Steve H. Forrest)

OPPOSITE BELOW: McLemore Avenue spanned the south end of South Yard, providing an ideal vantage point for photography. On November 3, 1974, a former Detroit, Toledo & Ironton GP9 assists a pair of ICG GP40s on a southbound piggyback train passing through South Yard. The DT&I unit was rebuilt by Paducah the following summer and became ICG GP10 #8095. (David M. Johnston)

ABOVE: When southbound intermodal train I01 passed through South Yard on September 28, 1990, there was still plenty of activity at the facility. But within three years, all of the work performed here was moved to Johnston Yard and all the yard tracks seen in this photo were pulled up. (Kirk Reynolds)

Two Freight Yards on the Passenger Main

The Memphis riverfront is now one of the city's premier tourist attractions, but during most of the 20th century the area was dominated by factories and warehouses served by Illinois Central, Union Railway of Memphis, Louisville & Nashville, Missouri Pacific, Rock Island and Frisco. The Illinois Central switching jobs that worked industries in this manufacturing district on the north side of town were based at IC's North Yard. Located about three miles north of Central Station near the east bank of the Wolf River, this facility was comprised of two groups of yard tracks that lay on either side of the main line.

A short distance south of Central Station, the Illinois Central passenger line crossed the tracks of the Missouri Pacific, the Rock Island and the Frisco at the city's busiest railroad junction, called Broadway by the IC, but known as IC Crossing on the other lines that shared the intersection. In spite of the volume of traffic through this location, all trains were required to stop. Movement of trains was governed by a switch tender, who operated a traffic light (the type used at street intersections, rather than a railroad-style signal) to dictate authority through the crossing.

Things slowed down at this important crossing even more in the mid-1970s when the switch tender's job was eliminated and stop signs were placed on all four sides of the crossing. Trains approaching the crossing were required to stop and, after determining there was no "train or engine on the conflicting routes, trains may proceed at YARD SPEED" (quoted from Illinois Central Gulf Delta Division timetable #3, April 25, 1976). The same procedure was dictated on the other railroads that crossed at ICG Crossing.

Just south of Broadway was the north end of Illinois Central's South Yard, referred to as Iowa Street Junction. South Yard marked the point where predecessor lines Mississippi & Tennessee, Yazoo & Mississippi Valley and Chesapeake, Ohio & Southwestern all came together. By the 1960s, Illinois Central operations through South Yard had all, but erased the vestiges of the ancestral roads that came into this part of Memphis from the north and south. After Illinois Central retired the last of its steam locomotives, the roundhouse at South Yard was closed. A facility for servicing passenger diesels was maintained at the yard, as was a small coach yard.

Broadway (or IC/ICG Crossing) was also an important interchange point between the Illinois Central/Illinois Central Gulf and

OPPOSITE ABOVE: At South Yard Junction, the former Mississippi & Tennessee and Yazoo & Mississippi Valley lines joined. The cantilever signal bridge in the upper left corner marks the junction. In October 1973, this southbound freight was heading down the old M&T line on its way to East Junction where it will turn onto the wye that will take it to Johnston Yard. The photographer was looking northwest from the 3rd Street overpass. (Steve H. Forrest)

OPPOSITE BELOW: As northbound ICG piggyback train #50 departed Johnston Yard on June 22, 1986, it passed the remains of the train order office at East Junction. The train is coming up the connecting track that IC crews called the City Wye, which linked the east end of Johnston Yard to the passenger main. (Scott D. Lindsey)

ABOVE: The departure of northbound "Fastback" train #50 from Johnston Yard was recorded by another photographer on a June evening in 1969. Compared to the photo at the bottom of the previous page, this view was taken a little farther south along the City Wye. The Grenada District is seen on the left where it met the route to Central Station. The overpass in the lower right side of the photo carried the City Wye over Interstate Route 55. During the summer of 1969 Illinois Central leased several F7 freight units from the Denver & Rio Grande Western Railroad to fill its motive power needs. Three D&RGW booster units assist IC E8 #4026 on this day's #50 as it headed for Chicago. When IC began running dedicated piggyback trains between Chicago and Memphis in 1968, surplus E-units were initially assigned to power the trains. As IC's piggyback business grew, it soon became apparent that the passenger units were ill-suited for this service. (Phil Gosney)

the other railroads that served Memphis. Missouri Pacific, Cotton Belt, Frisco, Rock Island and Southern brought their transfer runs through Broadway and into South Yard, while IC operated its transfer jobs to the yards of each of these roads out of both South Yard and Johnston Yard. Illinois Central Gulf concentrated its operations in Memphis at Johnston Yard during the 1980s and activity at South Yard decreased. By the early 1990s, all of the tracks had been removed from the yard.

President's Island is an industrial park that is located on the Mississippi River west of South Yard. Development of this industrial district (after the island was turned into a peninsula) began in the late 1940s. A reciprocal switching agreement was maintained between the Illinois Central, Frisco and Missouri Pacific to serve the customers in this district that were accessed through South Yard. Illinois Central Gulf eventually took over all the switching of the industries on President's Island.

At the southern end of South Yard, the former Yazoo & Mississippi Valley and Mississippi & Tennessee lines diverged at South Yard Junction (called Y&MV Junction into the late 1940s). The Y&MV was used for freight traffic and headed in a southwesterly direction toward West Junction at the western end of Johnston Yard. The old M&T line ran southward to East Junction where a bridge carried it over the tracks of IC's belt line around the city. Beyond East Junction, this route became the Grenada District and carried all Chicago-New Orleans passenger schedules south of Memphis.

The Freight Bypass

As the 19th century drew to a close, Illinois Central's main line along Memphis' riverfront was crowded with a flood of passenger and freight trains making their way through the city. Adding to the congestion were the numerous switching jobs that worked the industries and warehouses along the line. North and South yards were operating at capacity and a steep grade between the yards impeded the movement of heavy trains. During the steam era, pusher engines were required to assist southbound freights between Poplar Street and Central Station. Expanding the existing yards and easing the grade between them was deemed to be too expensive. The solution turned out to be construction of an entirely new yard and a freight-only thoroughfare that would bypass the congested city.

The project was undertaken in four stages. The first component to be built was a new freight classification yard south of the city limits, its location chosen to place it between the Y&MV and IC's Grenada District. Construction of Nonconnah Yard (named for nearby Nonconnah Creek) began in 1903 and the new yard went into operation January 1904. Due to the remote location of the new yard and the lack of public transit to it, the railroad ran an employee shuttle train (known as "The Hoodlum") from South Yard to Nonconnah Yard.

Work on the first segment of the new belt line, called the North Diagonal, began in 1905. It extended 7.44 miles between Woodstock, where it joined IC's main line, and Leewood. Arrangements were made with the Louisville & Nashville that would allow Illinois Central trains to operate over L&N's line between Leewood and Aulon, a distance of about two miles. This double-track North Diagonal was completed 1907. Illinois Central's Hollywood Yard, situated just north of the L&N crossing at Leewood, served industries on the city's east side.

The next improvement built was a new cut-off between the western end of Nonconnah Yard (called West Junction) and Lake View, Mississippi, a distance of 6.35 miles. This new track came to be known as the High Line while the original Y&MV main was called the Low Line. Grading started in 1906 and the line was opened in the fall of 1907.

The South Diagonal was the final element of IC's belt line around Memphis to be installed. The 6.81-mile stretch of double track ran from Aulon to East Junction at the eastern end of Nonconnah Yard. Along the way, there were grade separations with two other railroads; the belt line passed under Southern Railway and over the Frisco. Work started in March 1907 and was completed June 1, 1908. Most of Illinois Central's Chicago-New Orleans freight traffic was redirected around Memphis on the new belt line, though some freight schedules continued to run down the passenger main through town.

BELOW: Another perspective of East Junction is seen in this photo as southbound intermodal train #51 comes down the City Wye into Johnston Yard on January 4, 1976. The first two units in the engine consist were both among the last new locomotives purchased by the ICG and were named for notable figures in IC/GM&O history. GP38-2 #9629 was named for Edward T. Jeffery, an IC officer in the late 1800s, while SD40-2 #6030 carried the name of Floyd Mays. Mr. Mays was the IC's chief mechanical officer who managed the rebuilding of the IC's steam fleet at Paducah in the 1930s and 1940s. (Steve H. Forrest)

OPPOSITE ABOVE: Illinois Central served a number of industries adjacent to its freight bypass on the east side of Memphis. Cars for these customers were handled through Hollywood Yard, which was located just north of where the IC crossed the Louisville & Nashville's North Memphis main at Leewood. This southbound freight is passing the yard and is about to cross the L&N in November 1975. From Leewood to Aulon, the train will use trackage rights over the L&N. (Steve H. Forrest)

OPPOSITE BELOW: In February 1976, an ICG train rolls southward under the Southern Railway and Southern Avenue. In the background is Mid-South Coliseum and, to the right, Liberty Stadium. (Steve H. Forrest)

OPPOSITE ABOVE: A northbound ICG train with a classic trio of Geeps is about to pass the L&N "RS" operator's office at Leewood in July 1974. The train is on the L&N track, but will be back on the IC when it passes Leewood. (Steve H. Forrest)

OPPOSITE BELOW: The south end of Illinois Central's freight line around Memphis connected to the east end of Johnston Yard at A Yard Junction. In this photo looking east from the Third Street overpass on October 19, 1975, a northbound train (in the foreground) is crossing Nonconnah Creek as it departs the yard while another has come down the Hollywood District and is waiting to enter the yard. The Grenada District, which is mostly obscured by trees in this view, crossed over the belt line on a bridge in the distance. The wye track turning to the left in the center of the photo leads northward to East Junction where it connects with the passenger main through town. The track turning to the right in front of the operator's office was called the Grenada Wye and allowed trains leaving the yard to go south to the Grenada District. (David M. Johnston)

ABOVE: Of all the railroads serving Memphis, the Illinois Central handled the most traffic and it took a lot of people to get the job done. How many people? According to this sign erected at Johnston Yard in the 1940s, 4,000 employees. The sign was still standing in November 1974, but by then the number of Memphis citizens working for the Illinois Central Gulf had decreased significantly. (Steve H. Forrest)

Freight Operations at Memphis

Nonconnah Yard was originally comprised of four smaller yards with two rider humps (which required a brakeman to ride each car down the hump and apply the brakes when the car reached its proper track). Southbound traffic came into "B" yard and was classified over the hump to "C" yard while northbound trains arrived at "D" yard and were humped into "A" yard. Illinois Central's freight traffic through Memphis continued to grow in the years following the opening of the yard, necessitating an expansion that was finished in the summer of 1914.

After World War II, the decision was made to rebuild Nonconnah Yard into a flat switching operation. As work began in 1947, both humps were removed, and the area was leveled. Yards "A" and "B" were joined to form the new "A" yard, which would handle northbound trains. The "C" yard was expanded to classify southbound traffic, claiming some of the land occupied by "D" yard in the process. The job was finished in 1949 and the facility was renamed Johnston Yard after the railroad's president.

The majority of freight schedules operating north or south out of Memphis either originated or terminated at Johnston Yard. In 1961, the following IC mainline freight schedules served Johnston Yard:

Southbound

CN-1	Chicago (Markham Yard)-New Orleans
CN-5	Chicago (Congress Street Yard)-New Orleans
SN-3	St. Louis-New Orleans
SM-1	St. Louis-Memphis
LM-3	Louisville-Memphis
MJ-3	Memphis-Jackson, Mississippi
MV-3	Memphis-Vicksburg

Northbound

NC-2	New Orleans-Chicago (Congress Street Yard)
NC-6	New Orleans-Chicago (Congress Street Yard)
MI-2	Memphis-Indianapolis
MS-2	Memphis-St. Louis
ML-4	Memphis-Louisville
BM-2	Baton Rouge-Memphis

When IC commenced its trailer-on-flatcar service between Chicago and Memphis in the summer of 1955, a single loading ramp located north of "C" Yard served as the southern terminal for this new type of business. Piggyback service expanded across Illinois Central's territory over the next few years and by 1963 Johnston Yard's intermodal facility had grown to four tracks. In addition, new automobiles were also being unloaded from auto rack cars at the facility.

Following the success of Illinois Central's first dedicated intermodal schedules, operating between Chicago and Memphis, a second pair of TOFC trains (#55 and #56) went to work between Memphis and New Orleans in 1969. Johnston Yard's intermodal operation received a substantial upgrade in 1972 with the addition of four run-through tracks and new unloading equipment that replaced the old "circus loading" method of putting trailers on flat cars.

Freight and intermodal trains operating into, out of or through Johnston Yard in 1977 consisted of the following schedules:

Southbound

CM-1	Chicago-Memphis
CM-7	Chicago-Memphis
CN-5	Chicago-New Orleans
JFM	Jackson, Tennessee-Memphis
IM-1	Indianapolis-Memphis
SM-3	East St. Louis-Memphis
SM-5	East St. Louis-Memphis
LM-1	Louisville-Memphis
LM-7	Louisville-Memphis
MJ-3	Memphis-Jackson, Mississippi
MM-1	Memphis-McComb, Mississippi
MN-3	Memphis-New Orleans
MN-5	Memphis-New Orleans
51	Chicago IMX (Intermodal Exchange)-New Orleans
55	Memphis-Jackson, Mississippi

BELOW: Even after the Illinois Central's transition to diesels was completed, the roundhouse at Johnston Yard remained active. On a night during May 1974, four ex-Illinois Central Geeps and a former Gulf, Mobile & Ohio GP35 were being serviced in the building. (Steve H. Forrest)

OPPOSITE ABOVE: The Illinois Central Gulf merger is evident in January 1974 at the Johnston Yard roundhouse as a trio of former Gulf, Mobile & Ohio units rests below the Illinois Central logo on a safety sign. (Steve H. Forrest)

OPPOSITE BELOW: The washing of freight locomotives is a practice that seems to have all but disappeared from the American railroad scene. But in November 1974 the wash rack at the Johnston Yard roundhouse was still operational and is seen here being put to good use. (Steve H. Forrest)

Northbound

NC-6   New Orleans-Chicago
GC-6   Geismar-Chicago
GS-2   Geismar-St. Louis
MFB   Memphis-Birmingham
MC-4   Memphis-Chicago
MS-2   Memphis-East St. Louis
MI-2   Memphis-Indianapolis
ML-2   Memphis-Louisville
ML-4   Memphis-Louisville
JM-4   Jackson, Mississippi-Memphis
BM-2   Baton Rouge-Memphis
NM-2   New Orleans-Memphis
NM-4   New Orleans-Memphis
50   Memphis-Chicago IMX
56   New Orleans-Memphis

Illinois Central Gulf introduced a new type of intermodal service when it launched its "Supermode" service between Oak Street Yard in Louisville and Johnston Yard in Memphis in September, 1981. Utilizing RoadRailer trailers (highway trailers that were also equipped with rail wheels) the dedicated trains covered the 370-mile route in 16 hours. The service operated for about a year and was discontinued in October, 1982.

Through the 1980s, several large segments of ICG lines on the southern end of the system were sold or abandoned. The smaller size of the railroad was reflected in this summary of schedules serving Johnston Yard in 1987:

Southbound

CN-5   Chicago-New Orleans
CM-1   Chicago-Memphis
CR-5   Champaign, IL-Memphis
SM-3   East St. Louis-Memphis
MG-5   Memphis-Geismar, Louisiana
51   Chicago IMX-New Orleans
53   Venice, Illinois-Memphis
55   Memphis-McComb, Mississippi

Northbound

NC-6   New Orleans-Chicago
MC-4   Memphis-Chicago
CR-6   Memphis-Champaign, Illinois
GS-2   Geismar, Louisiana-East St. Louis
MJM   Mobile-Memphis
50   New Orleans-Chicago IMX
52   Memphis-Venice, Illinois
54   McComb, Mississippi-Memphis

The frenetic pace at which American railroad companies were merging to form large systems had quickened in the 1980s. As Illinois Central Gulf became Illinois Central again, the other roads it connected with in Memphis were also being transformed. In 1956, Illinois Central connected with seven other railroads at Memphis. By 1996, IC had just four interchange partners in the Birthplace of Rock 'n Roll.

BELOW: This southbound ICG freight stopped at East Junction in December 1979 before receiving permission to enter Johnston Yard. The Grenada District crossed over the belt line on the silver bridge in the distance and the City Wye can be seen on the left side of the photo. A broader view of this end of East Junction can be seen in the bottom photo on Page 110. (Steve H. Forrest)

OPPOSITE ABOVE: Since Memphis was the mid-way point on IC's Chicago-New Orleans main line, most of the locomotives on the trains running into, out of or through the city were serviced at Johnston Yard. On this clear day in November 1974, there was plenty of activity at Johnston Yard's sand and fuel racks as engines were prepared for their next duties. (Steve H. Forrest)

OPPOSITE BELOW: Though Illinois Central's half-dozen ALCO C636s spent most of their lives on the Kentucky Division, a pair of them made an appearance at Johnston Yard in November 1974. (Steve H. Forrest)

Main Line of Mississippi

There were two Illinois Central main lines that reached southward from Memphis. Freight traffic was dispatched over the Tallahatchie District (part of IC's Yazoo & Mississippi Valley subsidiary) while passenger trains took the Grenada District. The varied geography of northwestern Mississippi dictated which route each class of train would traverse.

The Grenada District set a course through the hill country, crossing many streams and rivers along the way. Conversely, the Yazoo & Mississippi Valley main lines that paralleled it to the west ran across the comparatively level Mississippi Delta, making those lines better suited to handling freight trains. So the Grenada line was the route of choice for the shorter and faster passenger trains. When IC began operating dedicated intermodal trains (which were somewhat lighter than conventional freight trains) to New Orleans in 1969, they were also dispatched over the passenger route.

When Amtrak took over operation of IC's Chicago-New Orleans passenger service in 1971, the route that the remaining schedule took between Memphis and Jackson, Mississippi continued to be over the Grenada District. In the early 1990s, the "new" Illinois Central had rebuilt the old Y&MV route between Memphis and Jackson with welded rail and centralized traffic control. By then, the only trains other than Amtrak using the Grenada route were local freights. Illinois Central and Amtrak changed the Memphis-Jackson route for the "City of New Orleans" trains from the Grenada line to the former Y&MV in September 1995.

The Grenada District had been the Mississippi & Tennessee Railroad before it was brought into the Illinois Central fold in 1889. The M&T connected with IC's original southern main line, the Mississippi Central, at Grenada. With Illinois Central's procurement of the Chesapeake, Ohio & Southwestern in 1896, the former M&T became part of IC's new Chicago-New Orleans route that ran through Memphis.

ABOVE: The Durant Turn, ICG trains #43 and #44, was a local that worked the Grenada District south from Grenada to Durant. It has finished its work for the day and is shown returning to the yard at Grenada on August 16, 1986. The train's conductor is walking across the main track to turn in his paperwork at the depot, seen on the right side of the photo. This station, built as a single-story structure, was extensively renovated in 1925 with a second story added to it. It continues to serve its original purpose as offices for the Grenada Railway, the short line that took over the operation of the former Grenada District. (Scott D. Lindsey)

OPPOSITE: It's train time at Winona, Mississippi, on the evening of August 26, 1976, and folks are gathering at the station in anticipation of the arrival of northbound Amtrak train #58, "The Panama Limited," from New Orleans. Today's train is led by two General Electric P30CHs, which were less than a year old when this scene was recorded. (Two photos, Mike McBride)

OPPOSITE ABOVE: Though the population of Durant, Mississippi, never exceeded 3,000, the Illinois Central deemed the community worthy of a substantial brick depot where the railroad's most prestigious passenger trains called every day. Brakeshoe smoke surrounds the northbound "City of New Orleans" as it eases to a stop at the Durant depot on this summer morning in the late 1960s. (Dennis E. Conniff)

OPPOSITE BELOW: Illinois Central train #2, "The City of New Orleans," departed Jackson, Mississippi, just minutes ago and is seen racing northward toward Memphis past Ridgeland on the morning of October 26, 1969. This community is a northern suburb of the capital city and this once-rural view from the Natchez Trace Parkway overpass is now dominated by urban development. The railroad seen here became Canadian National's Canton Subdivision, which serves Nissan auto and truck assembly plants at Canton. Solid trains of auto carriers have replaced the streamliners through Ridgeland. (Dennis E. Conniff)

ABOVE: The IC made a genuine effort to build its intermodal traffic from the time it entered the market in the mid-1950s up through the merger. When this photo was taken at the Kosciusko freight house on May 12, 1974, the ICG was operating 68 TOFC ramps across the system, many at facilities as small as this. The presence of the Norfolk & Western piggyback trailer and the empty TOFC flatcar to the left indicate this ramp was still active at this time, but the ICG would close this and several other smaller intermodal ramps in the next few years. (Dennis E. Conniff)

Initially, the Grenada and Water Valley districts met about a mile north of the Grenada depot at Memphis Junction. In 1947, construction of Grenada Dam, part of a flood control project, began. Grenada Lake, the reservoir that the new dam would form, would cover several miles of the Water Valley District. About a dozen miles of the line were relocated and the junction with the Grenada District moved north about 4.5 miles. It was renamed W.V. Junction.

The only notable railroad that Illinois Central encountered between Memphis and Jackson was the Columbus & Greenville Railway. The C&G rambled across northern Mississippi from its eastern terminus at Columbus (where it interchanged with Southern Railway, Frisco and Gulf, Mobile & Ohio) to Greenville on the Mississippi River. Along the way, it crossed Illinois Central lines at six locations. The C&G crossed the Water Valley District at Winona, Mississippi.

Operating in a region where economic opportunities were hard to come by and flooding was a recurring problem, Columbus & Greenville managed to hold its own as an independent line for more than 40 years. But by the late 1960s, the road had fallen upon hard times. In 1969, its owners asked the Interstate Commerce Commission to include it in the imminent IC/GM&O merger. The

request was approved, and the C&G became part of the Illinois Central Gulf on September 29, 1972.

At the time of the acquisition, the Columbus & Greenville was in pretty sad shape. Unfortunately, the attention of the line's new owners was focused elsewhere as they melded the former IC and GM&O properties into a unified rail network. As service on the former C&G declined further during 1973, local business leaders and investors entered negotiations with ICG to buy the railroad. Illinois Central Gulf sold the former C&G to local owners on October 29, 1975.

Tchula and Aberdeen Districts

Two secondary Illinois Central lines connected with what had been the southern end of the Water Valley District. The Tchula District linked the Water Valley District at Durant to IC's Yazoo District at Gwin. This district survived intact until 1978 when the section from Gwin to Lexington was torn up. The rest of the line between Lexington and Durant was abandoned in early 1982.

The other branch was the Aberdeen District, extending 106 miles from Aberdeen Junction, on the south side of Durant to Aberdeen, Mississippi. Along the way, the district crossed two

Gulf, Mobile & Ohio lines at Ackerman and West Point (where it also crossed the Columbus & Greenville) and connected with a GM&O branch at Starkville. At Aberdeen, the district connected with the Frisco line from Amory, Mississippi, to Pensacola, Florida. In the days of steam, IC owned an isolated eight-mile branch, which connected with the Frisco 45 miles east of Amory at Winfield, Alabama; Illinois Central trains had trackage rights over the SLSF between Aberdeen and Winfield. The Winfield District was a major source of coal for the south end of the IC, making the Aberdeen District quite busy. After Illinois Central converted to diesel power, the Winfield District was sold to the Frisco.

In 1981, Illinois Central Gulf obtained permission to abandon the middle section of the Aberdeen District between Kosciusko and Fentress. The northern end of the district was sold to L. B. Foster Company in 1985 and became part of Gulf & Mississippi Rail Corporation. The southern end of the Aberdeen District between Aberdeen Junction and Kosciusko was sold in 1998 to the Mississippi Department of Transportation. The line was then leased to the Kosciusko Southwestern Railway.

In April 1967, the southern end of the Water Valley District (94 miles between Grenada and Canton) was consolidated into the Grenada District. This moved the southern end of the Grenada District down to Canton where it met the Canton District.

The Canton District constituted the middle segment of the Memphis-New Orleans main line. The northern 25 miles of the district was a single-track line that carried mostly passenger trains. South of Jackson to McComb, Mississippi, it was a double-track thoroughfare for both passenger and freight traffic. The Canton District was a straight, fast piece of railroad with few speed restrictions.

Jackson, Mississippi

In addition to being the capitol of the Magnolia State, Jackson was Illinois Central's most important terminal between Memphis and New Orleans. Two busy IC main lines intersected at Jackson. The Canton District constituted IC's main route through Jackson while the Meridian District was part of the railroad's east-west route between Meridian, Mississippi, and Shreveport, Louisiana.

BELOW: A couple of GP10s are waiting for their next assignment by the Aberdeen depot on June 21, 1985. About three weeks after this photo was taken, the Aberdeen District between Ackerman and Aberdeen became part of the Gulf & Mississippi Railroad. This line was eventually incorporated into the Kansas City Southern system, which serves a large chemical plant on the southwest side of town. (Scott D. Lindsey)

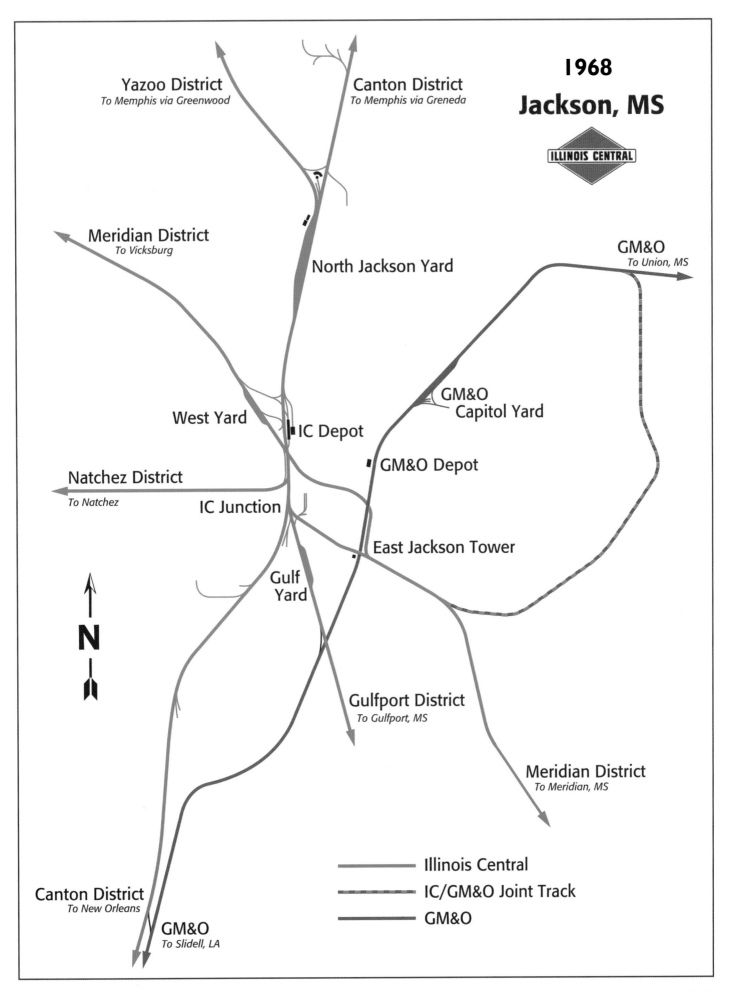

1968
Jackson, MS

ILLINOIS CENTRAL

Yazoo District
To Memphis via Greenwood

Canton District
To Memphis via Greneda

Meridian District
To Vicksburg

North Jackson Yard

GM&O
To Union, MS

West Yard

GM&O
Capitol Yard

IC Depot

GM&O Depot

Natchez District
To Natchez

IC Junction

East Jackson Tower

Gulf
Yard

N

Gulfport District
To Gulfport, MS

Meridian District
To Meridian, MS

Illinois Central

IC/GM&O Joint Track

Canton District
To New Orleans

GM&O
To Slidell, LA

GM&O

BELOW: A worker replaces a burned-out bulb in one of the number boards on RDC-2, a rail defect detector car, while it is parked on a side track at the Jackson passenger station on November 6, 1971. Illinois Central built two of these two-car units to Association of American Railroads specifications, the first in 1943 and another in 1945. These cars originally wore IC's brown-and-orange passenger paint scheme but were later repainted into IC's orange-and-white scheme. (Dennis E. Conniff)

OPPOSITE ABOVE: The Woodrow Wilson Avenue viaduct spans the northern end of Jackson's North Yard and provides this vista. Northbound train NM-4 has stopped south of the bridge in front of the yard office (out of the picture to the left), as the crew confers before departing for Memphis on September 1, 1986. (Scott D. Lindsey)

OPPOSITE BELOW: Southbound train #3, the "Louisiane," runs past North Jackson Yard in the mid-1960s. The train's consist was a mix of the new and the old. Up front was an A-B set of E-units, both about a decade old. Behind them was a Flexi-Van car carrying a single container. Flexi-Vans were used by the Illinois Central during the early 1960s to carry mail. The rest of the train was made up of heavyweight cars that included a Railway Post Office, a baggage car and four coaches. The Woodrow Wilson Avenue bridge over the IC and Mill Street, which runs alongside the tracks, can be seen in the background. Beyond it, above the rear of the train, is another relic of the past, the massive steel coaling tower that stood at the junction of the Canton and Yazoo Districts. A few concrete coal docks still stand today along the former IC, but the North Jackson facility succumbed to the scrapper's torch not long after this photo was taken. (Dennis E. Conniff)

OPPOSITE ABOVE: Though it was the busiest station between Memphis and New Orleans, the new facility opened at Jackson in 1925 was compact and efficient. This view of the station's facade on Capitol St. taken on October 17, 1969, reveals an unpretentious structure. Mail and express shipments were handled at docks along Mill St., which ran northward from the intersection at the right side of the photo. The property eventually passed to Canadian National, who sold it to the City of Jackson in 2003. It has been renovated and serves as the city's Amtrak station and terminal for local transit and intercity buses. (Dennis E. Conniff)

OPPOSITE BELOW: A southbound IC freight led by a pair of GP9s passes the platforms at Jackson's station in August 1969. In the shadows of the canopy over the platform to the right, the northbound "City of New Orleans" has made its arrival, scheduled for 10:30 a.m. The photographer was standing above the West Pearl Street overpass. Just behind him was where the A&V freight line through the city ran beneath the IC. In 1926, the IC elevated its main line through Jackson to eliminate several busy street crossings and provide a modern passenger station for the city. It was one of many costly, but necessary projects that the railroad completed that year, among them the Chicago improvements and the Edgewood Cutoff. The two engines on the southbound freight were delivered in January 1956 and would both be remanufactured at Paducah. The lead engine, #9171, was rebuilt a couple of years after this photo was taken to become GP10 #8171. The second unit, #9136, rolled out a decade later in January 1981 as ICG GP11 #8751. (Jim Boyd)

ABOVE: Observation-Bar-Lounge car #3305 was a common sight on the rear of the "City of New Orleans," seen here as train #2 departs Jackson on September 26, 1968. When World War II ended, the Illinois Central, like every other major railroad, needed plenty of new passenger trains. As the car builders transitioned back to civilian production, their orders for new lightweight, streamlined equipment piled up. The backlog of orders meant IC couldn't get new cars quickly enough to fill all its needs. To provide diners, lounge and other types of streamlined equipment, the railroad's Burnside Shop near Chicago remanufactured several old heavyweight coaches into cars that were completely new from the frame up. This car was originally coach #2188, built by Pullman in 1916. (Dennis E. Conniff)

There were also two IC branches that ran southward from the city: one to Natchez, Mississippi, and the other to Gulfport, Mississippi.

The Meridian District from Vicksburg connected with the Canton District north of downtown Jackson. The other side of the Meridian District, from Meridian, joined the Canton District about a half-mile south of the Vicksburg line junction. Meridian District trains travelling through Jackson did so by turning onto the Canton District and negotiating a series of crossovers to reach the connection to the other side of the Meridian District. This cumbersome arrangement came about in 1926 when Illinois Central elevated its tracks through Jackson to eliminate several grade crossings. A new passenger station with track-level platforms was part of the improvement project.

Illinois Central's subsidiary Yazoo & Mississippi Valley took control of the Alabama & Vicksburg, the railroad that became the Meridian District, in early 1926. Freight trains on the former A&V used a track at ground level to pass under the elevated tracks of the Canton District. In order for Meridian District passenger trains to reach the platforms of the new station, elevated connecting tracks to the lines from Meridian and Vicksburg were built. Decades later, the ground-level freight line was abandoned, and all Meridian District traffic went over the elevated tracks through downtown Jackson.

North Yard was Illinois Central's freight classification yard at Jackson, located north of the city. The Yazoo District, the freight line from Memphis, joined the Canton District at the north end of the yard.

One of North Yard's principal functions was to relay traffic between Chicago/Memphis-New Orleans trains and those on the Meridian District and the branches to Gulfport and Natchez. At one time, there was another yard at Jackson involved with the exchange of cars between Meridian District and mainline freight schedules. West Yard was located west of downtown on the line to Vicksburg. Meridian District trains set out and picked up cars at West Yard for Jackson, Memphis, Chicago and other points on the main line. Switch engines would shuttle the blocks of cars between the two yards. In 1954, four tracks were added to North Yard and West Yard was closed.

Branches to Natchez and Gulfport

One of the branches that IC operated out of Jackson was the Natchez District. Reaching 98 miles to Natchez on the Mississippi River, the district was a Y&MV property. It diverged from the New Orleans main line a few city blocks south of Jackson's passenger station. On its way to Natchez, the line crossed just one other railroad, IC's Vicksburg District (part of Y&MV's Memphis-New Orleans route) at Harriston.

In April 1979, a large section of the Natchez District west of Harriston was abandoned leaving a short branch that was served from the Vicksburg District. Later that year, another long segment of the Natchez District reaching eastward from Harriston was also abandoned. Most of the remaining segment of the Natchez District south of Jackson was abandoned in 1981.

The other branch that extended southward from Jackson was the Gulfport District. It stretched 160 miles to reach its namesake city on Mississippi's Gulf Coast. The line was built as the Gulf & Ship Island Railroad, completed in 1900. Illinois Central bought the G&SI in 1925, giving it access to a second port on the Gulf Coast.

The line to Gulfport began just south of the junction where the Meridian District split from the Canton District and turned east toward Meridian. There was a small yard south of this junction called Gulf Yard. About a mile beyond Gulf Yard, the Gulfport District crossed Jackson's "other" railroad. Gulf, Mobile & Ohio's route between New Orleans and Union, Mississippi, passed through Jackson, crossing IC's Gulfport and Meridian districts on the way.

There were two branches that diverged off the Gulfport District. The Columbia District travelled southward 56 miles from Mendenhall to Columbia, Mississippi, where it met the shortline Fernwood, Columbia & Gulf Railroad and a branch of the Gulf, Mobile & Ohio. At one time, this line continued south and then east from Columbia, crossing the Southern Railway at Lumberton and rejoining the G&SI main line at Maxie. In 1982, the last remaining portion of the Columbia District, 28 miles between Columbia and the crossing with the Central District (former Mississippi Central) at Silver Creek, was sold to the Marion County Railroad Authority. This line was operated under several different names before finally being abandoned.

BELOW: Train #4, the northbound "Louisiane," paused at Jackson on December 30, 1961. Today's train requires at least three locomotives: E6 #4003 is on the point, assisted by E7 #4004 and an unidentified E8. The northbound "Louisiane" would be discontinued between Memphis and New Orleans on March 11, 1967. (Louis A. Marre)

OPPOSITE ABOVE: On April 10, 1998, southbound intermodal train I01 finished its work at North Jackson Yard and passed through the city on its way to New Orleans. It is seen at Switchtender, the junction south of the Jackson passenger station where IC's lines to Meridian, Gulfport and Natchez all split off the main line. The track curving off to the left was the Natchez District, while the Meridian District is on the other side of the main line. After its acquisition of MidSouth Rail, Kansas City Southern partnered with Norfolk Southern to develop the old A&V into a Dallas-Atlanta intermodal corridor. KCS trains use Canadian National tracks for about a mile between Switchtender and the junction north of the station where the KCS line to Shreveport turns west. (David Patch)

OPPOSITE BELOW: This earlier view of Switchtender, taken from a different perspective on May 21, 1976, shows a northbound ICG freight heading for North Jackson Yard. The first car behind the engines appears to be carrying crossties while the flatcars trailing it carry pulpwood heading for a paper mill. (Joseph R. Quinn, David P. Oroszi collection)

The Laurel District headed eastward from Saratoga 41 miles to reach Laurel and connections with the main lines of the Southern Railway and Gulf, Mobile & Ohio. Illinois Central Gulf abandoned the district east of Taylorsville between 1979 and 1983. The remainder of the district between Saratoga and Taylorsville became IC's Taylorsville District in the 1990s.

The Gulfport District crossed three other railroads at Hattiesburg. From north to south, the first was the Mississippi Central Railroad. Not to be confused with the ancestral Mississippi Central which became part of Illinois Central's southern main line, this Mississippi Central (MSC) had started out as a logging road in the 1890s. It continued to grow and, by 1908, stretched across Mississippi from Hattiesburg to Natchez. The Mississippi Central and its connection on the west side of the Mississippi River at Natchez, the Louisiana Midland, were nicknamed the Natchez Route. The Illinois Central purchased both of these railroads in 1967. The MSC became IC's Central District and the Louisiana Midland was named the Midland District.

The next line the Gulfport District crossed was Hattiesburg's most prominent railroad, Southern Railway subsidiary New Orleans & Northeastern. This was a part of Southern's busy main line connecting Birmingham and New Orleans.

Illinois Central's Bell Yard was located just north of the crossing with Hattiesburg's third railroad, the Bonhomie & Hattiesburg Southern. The 27-mile B&HS was bought by Illinois Central Gulf on August 31, 1972, and became ICG's Beaumont District.

The Gulfport District appropriately ended at the shores of the Gulf of Mexico in Gulfport, Mississippi. Illinois Central's North Yard was situated a short distance north of the crossing and connection with the Louisville & Nashville's New Orleans-Mobile main line. The city's passenger station was located in the southeast corner of the crossing and served the trains of both railroads. The Illinois Central marketing department promoted Gulfport and the Mississippi Gulf Coast as a vacation destination and a Chicago-Gulfport sleeper ran until passenger service to Gulfport was discontinued in 1950.

BELOW: The small town of Raymond, Mississippi, (about 15 miles west of Jackson) was graced with this impressive two-story depot. Though it looks rather neglected in this November 1971 photo, it was saved and placed on the National Register of Historic Places in 1986. (Frank E. Ardrey, Jr., David P. Oroszi collection)

OPPOSITE ABOVE: Illinois Central GP9 #9333 crosses the lead to the Southern Railway's yard at Hattiesburg, Mississippi, with a couple of wood racks full of pulpwood and a caboose on its way to Bell Yard on November 16, 1974. (Michael M. Palmieri)

OPPOSITE BELOW: Southbound IC train JAMO-27 (Jackson, MS-Mobile, AL) arrives at the south end of Bell Yard in Hattiesburg on April 27, 1994. The post-1988 Illinois Central retained its route to Mobile by piecing together remaining sections of the Gulf & Ship Island, Bonhomie & Hattiesburg Southern and Gulf, Mobile & Northern. (Mike Abalos)

OPPOSITE ABOVE: With its acquisition of the Gulf & Ship Island in 1925, the IC added Gulfport as a vacation destination in its advertising. The Louisville & Nashville shared a station with the IC where the lines crossed. On April 22, 1985, a lone ICG GP10 was parked north of the L&N (by then, Seaboard System) diamond at Gulfport. Even though there is no passenger service through the city on either line, the station, which was behind the photographer, has been preserved. (Michael M. Palmieri)

OPPOSITE BELOW: On a May morning in 1961, an SW900 and a pair of GP9s were parked at the small diesel servicing facility at Gulfport. The switcher would be rebuilt at Paducah into an unpowered slug, ICG #58, in 1981. The two GP9s, #9328 and #9121, would be converted into IC GP10s #8328 and #8121 respectively. (Charles Laird Sr., David P. Oroszi collection)

ABOVE: Once upon a time when a railroad had a train wreck, they didn't call in an outside contractor to clean up the mess; they took care of it themselves. Still coal-fired in April 1969, Illinois Central wreck derrick X92 (assigned to McComb, Mississippi) is untangling the mess at Terry, Mississippi. (Dennis E. Conniff)

In addition to serving several Gulfport industries, IC also performed all of the switching at the city's port. The harbor and wharves were initially developed by the Gulf & Ship Island, but were later sold to the State of Mississippi. In 1979, ICG built a 14-mile branch to serve a new DuPont titanium oxide plant at the north end of Bay St. Louis. The line began just north of Gulfport Yard and ran west to Delisle, Mississippi.

In March 1986, Illinois Central Gulf sold its Meridian-Shreveport line to MidSouth Rail Corporation. The sale also included the Hattiesburg-Gulfport section of the Gulfport District. Illinois Central Gulf retained the Jackson-Hattiesburg portion of the Gulfport District and combined it with the Beaumont District and sections of former Gulf, Mobile & Ohio track. The combination created a new Jackson-Mobile route called the Beaumont District, which remained part of the post-ICG Illinois Central.

Jackson-New Orleans

The Canton District continued southward from Jackson. While Illinois Central had separate single-track passenger and freight lines between Memphis and Jackson, the railroad was dou-

ble track all the way from Jackson to New Orleans for most of the 20th century.

The Canton District crossed the Central District (former Mississippi Central Railroad) at Brookhaven, 54 miles south of Jackson. Two large paper mills, one at Ferguson, Mississippi, (east of Brookhaven) and the other at Natchez, provided a steady flow of traffic that made the Central District a profitable stretch of railroad. The western segment of the Natchez Route, the Midland District, was a different story. It had very little business once the IC rerouted the Natchez Route's Meridian-Shreveport traffic over the more direct route through Jackson. The Midland District was sold by ICG in 1974.

Of the two routes for Jackson-Natchez traffic, the Central District came to be favored over the Natchez District. Though the Natchez District was more direct than sending the traffic via Brookhaven, the lack of customers along the line was a factor in ICG's decision to abandon it.

The Canton District joined with the McComb District at McComb, Mississippi, about 80 miles south of Jackson and 100 miles north of New Orleans. The town was founded in 1872 by Henry S. McComb, president of the New Orleans, Jackson &

Great Northern Railroad. With land prices and labor costs lower in rural Mississippi than in New Orleans, McComb wanted to move the NOJ&GN's locomotive and car shops out of the Crescent City.

Illinois Central was the town's biggest employer. One of the railroad's two freight car shops was located at McComb (the other was at Centralia, Illinois). Other facilities included a roundhouse, a coal dock and icing platform. South Yard straddled the main line a couple of miles south of town. Before Mays Yard was built north of New Orleans, the yard at McComb classified most of the southbound traffic.

Through the years, the railroad's presence in McComb gradually diminished. When the steam era ended, a diesel refueling facility replaced the roundhouse. The structure was torn down in the early 1950s, but the turntable remained in use into the mid-1980s. As ICG became a smaller railroad, there were fewer cars to repair and the car shops were closed in 1985.

A few miles south of McComb, the Fernwood District ran eastward from its junction with the McComb District. This district had been the Fernwood, Columbia & Gulf, a short line whose owners had petitioned to be included in the Illinois Central Gulf merger. The 44-mile railroad was absorbed on August 31, 1972, but it didn't last long as part of ICG. The eastern end of the district was abandoned in 1975 while the rest was pulled up in 1981.

As the McComb District crossed the Louisiana state line, it entered a region that abounded with farms that specialized in the cultivation of strawberries. From the first years of the 20th century into the 1960s, Illinois Central ran dedicated trains of express refrigerator cars that expedited the strawberries to northern markets. The ice bunkers of the cars would be filled at McComb before the cars were taken to their loading points in Louisiana. Once loaded, the trains were given priority over all other traffic. These trains were known as "Crimson Flyers" in reference to the color of the fruit they carried.

BELOW: In the 1980s, Amtrak's ubiquitous F40s were the regular power on the "City of New Orleans" while the train itself was made up of rolling stock from a variety of Amtrak's predecessors. When the southbound "City" pulled into Brookhaven, Mississippi, on August 31, 1986, the train's 12-car consist even included a dome car. Amtrak equipped its Chicago-New Orleans route with Superliner cars in March 1994. (Scott D. Lindsey)

OPPOSITE ABOVE: The three GP40s on this northbound train were running full throttle as they departed McComb, Mississippi, on the afternoon of November 1, 1978. These three engines were delivered as part of the IC's first order of GP40s in early 1966. Each would be rebuilt into a GP40r by VMV Enterprises at Paducah. The lead unit became IC #3104, one of the first engines to wear the paint scheme that was created for the soon-to-be independent IC in late 1987. The trailing units, #3028 and #3027, became #3115 and #3114 respectively. (Mark R. Demaline)

OPPOSITE BELOW: A hostler eases IC GP28 #9437 back towards the sand tower at the McComb engine facility on November 1, 1978. Only 16 GP28s were built for U.S. railroads and Illinois Central bought 3/4 of them. This particular engine would be sold to the Iowa Railroad in February 1983. The tall angular structure in the distance on the left side of the photo was the coaling tower for IC's roundhouse at McComb. (Mark R. Demaline)

OPPOSITE ABOVE: Years after the roundhouse at McComb was torn down, diesel maintenance continued at the old locomotive shop. On June 27, 1983, an SW14 and a GP10 were parked at the shop waiting to be serviced. Eventually, the shop was closed and the building demolished. The turntable was also removed and the pit filled in. The only structure related to steam locomotive maintenance that remains at McComb today is the concrete coaling tower that stands north of the Pearl River Avenue viaduct. (Jerry Sires)

OPPOSITE BELOW: This Bucyrus Erie wrecking derrick assigned to McComb had recently received a fresh paint job inside and out when it was photographed on November 1, 1978. (Mark R. Demaline)

ABOVE: In this view from the Pearl River Avenue bridge, northbound Illinois Central train #6, the "Panama Limited," slows to a stop at McComb on July 12, 1969. The locomotive shop can be seen in the background above the "Panama's" engine consist. The car shops are in the upper right corner of the photo. There was still plenty of activity at the car shops at the time with several bad order cars on tracks behind the passenger train awaiting their turn in the shop. (Dennis E. Conniff)

At Hammond, Louisiana, the Hammond District split off from the main line and headed west to Baton Rouge. Built as a part of the Baton Rouge, Hammond & Eastern Railroad, the line originally ran from Baton Rouge to Hammond, crossed the IC main line and continued to Covington, Louisiana, where it connected with the New Orleans-Great Northern. Before its construction was completed in 1908, the BRH&E came under the control of the Yazoo & Mississippi Valley.

In 1918, the BRH&E/IC crossing at Hammond was removed and connecting tracks to the Baton Rouge and Covington lines were laid. The Hammond-Covington segment was abandoned by IC in 1934, but the track wasn't removed for almost 40 years. This line became a pulpwood-hauling route, operated first by the Natalbany Lumber Company and then by the Gaylord Container Company and its successor, Crown Zellerbach Corporation. It was finally abandoned in the early 1970s.

The western section of the BRH&E carried on as IC's Hammond District. It became a crucial link between Illinois Central's main line and the Baton Rouge District. After the Second World War, industry developed rapidly along the Mississippi River from Baton Rouge southward. Many of the industrial plants along the river supplied valuable chemical traffic

to the Baton Rouge district. Much of that business was handled on the former Y&MV Memphis-New Orleans route.

In the late 1970s, ICG began to reroute traffic from the Baton Rouge-Vicksburg-Memphis line, sending it instead over the Hammond District and then northward on the main line. With the overhead traffic gone from the Baton Rouge-Memphis route, ICG abandoned most of it between 1981 and 1985.

At Pass Manchac, the railroad crossed a large channel that joins Lake Pontchartrain and Lake Maurepas. The New Orleans, Jackson & Great Northern built a long trestle across the Pass in 1854 with a wooden draw span to allow for the passage of boats between the lakes. This was succeeded by a wooden swing span, an iron swing span and then a steel swing span. This last span served for 68 years before being replaced with the current bascule truss bridge in 1972.

After crossing Pass Manchac, the McComb District began curving along the western shore of Lake Pontchartrain. This curve, over nine miles long, was the longest single railroad curve in the United States.

Illinois Central installed centralized traffic control on 37 miles of the McComb District between Oliver (just south of Hammond) and Skip (near the southern end of the district) in 1960. The instal-

OPPOSITE ABOVE: Amtrak had been running the nation's passenger trains for almost eight months when southbound train #59, the "Panama Limited," paused at McComb on November 28, 1971. Cars from other railroads were starting to show up in the train's consist and it was apparent that this was no longer the Illinois Central's "Panama Limited." (Dennis E. Conniff)

OPPOSITE BELOW: Illinois Central business car #9 was built by Pullman in 1917 for general passenger service. It was renumbered several times before ending up as office car #9. The car is seen parked south of the McComb station across the main line from the car shops on May 10, 1972. (Dennis E. Conniff)

ABOVE: Even though passenger service to Amite, Louisiana, ended in 1967, the town's depot was still standing when this southbound ICG freight passed by in May 1974. No longer needed by the railroad, the depot has been repurposed as the offices of the town's police department. (Tom Sink)

lation permitted IC to replace one of the main tracks with three controlled sidings that were each about two miles in length.

The McComb and Baton Rouge Districts converged at Orleans Junction to connect with IC's New Orleans District. For many years, the parallel Y&MV and IC main lines between Orleans Junction and downtown New Orleans were used as double track, with southbound traffic on the Y&MV and northbound on the IC. The arrangement ended with the decline of passenger traffic in the 1960s.

Kansas City Southern's subsidiary, Louisiana & Arkansas, also crossed the McComb District at Orleans Junction. The L&A paralleled the IC main line from Orleans Junction to downtown New Orleans. In 1985, a new connection was built on the Baton Rouge District just west of Orleans Junction that would allow KCS trains to use ICG tracks for about 6.5 miles to East Bridge Junction. After these changes were made, KCS abandoned its own parallel track through Kenner and Metairie.

New Orleans

While Chicago was the largest city served by Illinois Central, New Orleans was just as influential in defining the railroad's raison d'être. In the years prior to the Civil War, Chicago was growing rapidly and becoming a major port on the Great Lakes. Shipping on the Great Lakes (and railroads that were building across Ohio and Indiana to Chicago) provided Illinois farmers with a way to sell their produce in markets in the eastern states. But New Orleans was an ocean port that hosted the ships of many nations. Illinois Central's directors understood that providing a link between the railroad's southern terminus at Cairo and New Orleans would give merchants and farmers in Illinois access to foreign markets. To establish a reliable connection between Cairo and the Crescent City, IC put together its own fleet of riverboats.

After the Civil War, Illinois Central management knew that the railroad would have to grow to survive and they once again set

OPPOSITE ABOVE: Illinois Central's stately brick depot at Hammond, Louisiana, was completed in February 1912. When this photo was taken on June 14, 1972, it had been serving as an Amtrak facility for a little more than a year. After ICG decided to vacate the building in the 1980s, it was acquired and renovated by the city's chamber of commerce to accommodate offices and the city's Amtrak station. (R. M. Leach)

OPPOSITE BELOW: Six engines are leading northbound train NC-6 two miles south of Ponchatoula, Louisiana, on September 30, 1983. The three GP40s up front are the train's regular power while the three trailing six-axle units in the consist came south on a grain train and are now returning northward. (Michael M. Palmieri)

ABOVE: At Pass Manchac, the Illinois Central maintained a drawbridge to accommodate maritime traffic using the pass between Lake Pontchartrain and Lake Maurepas. On September 23, 1979, this empty grain train made its way northward across the long trestle. (Michael M. Palmieri)

their sights on New Orleans. While riverboats had largely been replaced by railroads, New Orleans was still the nation's second largest seaport. Illinois Central's acquisition of the New Orleans, Jackson & Great Northern and the Mississippi Central in 1877 enabled IC to provide its customers with access to this international port. Moreover, the purchase established the Chicago-New Orleans main line as Illinois Central's principal route.

About four miles east of Orleans Junction, the New Orleans District passed Mays Yard. When the United States entered World War II, Illinois Central's main freight yards were located in the city and along the riverfront. As wartime traffic increased, all those facilities were operating at full capacity and there was no room at any of the yards for expansion. To handle the additional traffic, the decision was made to build a new freight yard outside the city. Construction of Mays Yard began in April 1942 and was completed in early 1944. All of IC's road freights operating into and out of New Orleans terminated or originated at Mays Yard. Transfer runs shuttled traffic between Mays and the other four IC freight yards in the city: Stuyvesant, Levee, Poydras and Government yards.

At the eastern end of Mays Yard lay a small Southern Pacific Railroad yard, East Bridge Yard. After the Huey P. Long railroad/highway bridge over the Mississippi River opened in 1935, Southern Pacific moved its New Orleans interchange point with IC to this yard.

Just beyond the SP yard was East Bridge Junction. The tracks of the New Orleans Public Belt Railroad on the east end of the Huey P. Long Bridge (owned by the NOPB) met IC's New Orleans District on the south side of this junction. The two railroads ran side-by-side for about two miles to Southport Junction. At Southport Junction, the New Orleans District split and went two directions: one line went south to the riverfront while the other headed for the middle of the city. The NOPB also turned toward the riverfront at Southport interlocking and ran next to IC's line. The IC's little Southport Yard was just south of the interlocking and served customers in the vicinity.

The New Orleans District continued toward the heart of the city. There were two Illinois Central yards on this end of the district: Poydras Yard and Government Yard. Poydras Yard had been built by the New Orleans & Mississippi Valley, a predecessor of the Y&MV. It served nearby industries and shippers as well as IC's less-than-carload traffic for the city. The freight office located in a warehouse near Poydras Yard was the New Orleans terminal's nerve center where most of the clerical work was processed. Government Yard was used primarily for cleaning and maintaining passenger equipment operating into and out of IC's Union Station.

Union Station was Illinois Central's passenger station in New Orleans before New Orleans Union Passenger Terminal was built. It stood at the end of the New Orleans District on Rampart Street.

In addition to serving IC passenger trains, this depot also hosted passenger trains of the Yazoo & Mississippi Valley, Southern Pacific and Missouri Pacific.

Planning for a new passenger terminal that would replace IC's venerable Union Station (opened in 1892) and the city's four other passenger stations started in 1938. The war delayed those plans, but negotiations resumed in 1945. Construction of the new passenger station, New Orleans Union Passenger Terminal, was started in late 1951. The new station officially opened on May 1, 1954. It was built on much of the property once occupied by IC's Union Station and IC's Government Yard became NOUPT's car maintenance yard.

Southern Pacific and Texas & Pacific passenger trains came off of the Huey P. Long Bridge and joined those of the Illinois Central and Missouri Pacific's Gulf Coast Lines on the New Orleans District at East Bridge Junction. All these passenger trains travelled over the New Orleans District to Southport Junction where they diverged onto the New Orleans Union Passenger Terminal Western Connection. This connection used the right-of-way of a former KCS line. The New Orleans District east of

Southport Junction was abandoned and IC/ICG freight trains and transfer runs also used the NOUPT Western Connection to reach Poydras Yard until that facility closed in 1984.

South of Southport Junction, the other leg of the New Orleans District headed south, following the Mississippi River. Before Mays Yard was built, Stuyvesant Docks Yard was Illinois Central's main yard in New Orleans. Stuy Docks, as it was most commonly called, was a mile-long complex of wharves, rail yards and warehouses. The facility was located along the east bank of the Mississippi southwest of the city's central business district. The docks handled a wide range of imported commodities as well as export goods. When IC inaugurated intermodal service to New Orleans in June 1956, the piggyback ramp was established at Mays Yard. It was eventually relocated to Stuy Docks and remained there until IC's sale to Canadian National.

Illinois Central's Levee Yard was situated about 3 miles downriver from Stuyvesant Yard. Unlike Stuy Docks, Levee Yard handled only one commodity, bananas. Ships carrying bananas were unloaded at Thalia Street Wharf next to Levee Yard and the fruit was loaded into pre-cooled refrigerator cars. The cars had been

BELOW: After stopping at Manchac to pick up four more grain cars, the empty grain train continued northward. Here it is crossing the trestle over North Pass, another stream running between Lake Maurepas and Lake Pontchartrain. (Michael M. Palmieri)

OPPOSITE ABOVE: This southbound ICG grain train crossing Pass Manchac was captured on September 22, 1979. At the time, the grain trains usually ran with a caboose on each end as the power had to run around the train in Kenner, Louisiana, before heading up the former Y&MV line to the elevators along the Mississippi River. In 1985, a new connecting track was built at Kenner to expedite the movement of trains from the McComb District to the Baton Rouge District. (Michael M Palmieri)

OPPOSITE BELOW: The Bonnet Carre Spillway is a flood control operation about 12 miles west of New Orleans that allows overflow volume from the Mississippi River to be diverted to Lake Pontchartrain. When the U.S. Army Corps of Engineers constructed it in the 1930s, the Illinois Central and Kansas City Southern were required to build long trestles across the spillway. On August 13, 1975, Amtrak's northbound "Panama Limited" made its way across the long trestle that carried the McComb District over the spillway. (Jerry Dziedzic)

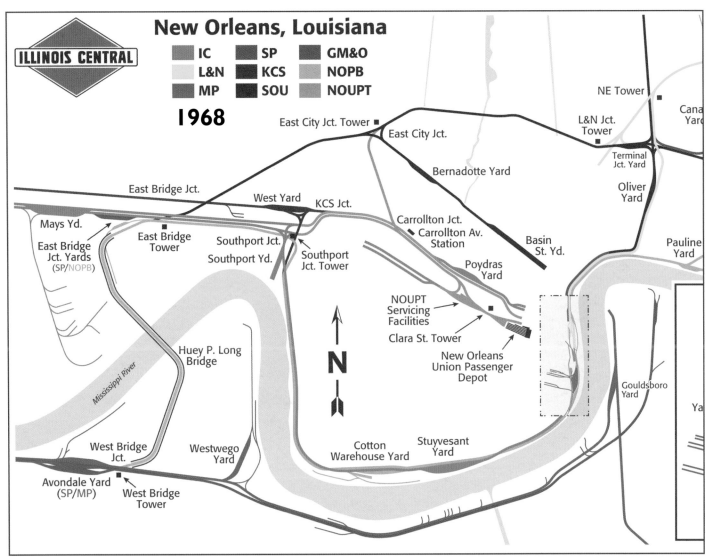

New Orleans, Louisiana

ILLINOIS CENTRAL

☐ IC	☐ SP	☐ GM&O			
☐ L&N	☐ KCS	☐ NOPB			
☐ MP	☐ SOU	☐ NOUPT			

1968

NE Tower

L&N Jct. Tower

Canal Yard

East City Jct. Tower

East City Jct.

Terminal Jct. Yard

Bernadotte Yard

Oliver Yard

East Bridge Jct.

West Yard

KCS Jct.

Carrollton Jct.

Carrollton Av. Station

Basin St. Yd.

Pauline Yard

Mays Yd.

East Bridge Tower

Southport Jct.

Southport Jct. Tower

Poydras Yard

East Bridge Jct. Yards (SP/NOPB)

Southport Yd.

NOUPT Servicing Facilities

Clara St. Tower

New Orleans Union Passenger Depot

Gouldsboro Yard

Huey P. Long Bridge

Mississippi River

N

West Bridge Jct.

Westwego Yard

Cotton Warehouse Yard

Stuyvesant Yard

Avondale Yard (SP/MP)

West Bridge Tower

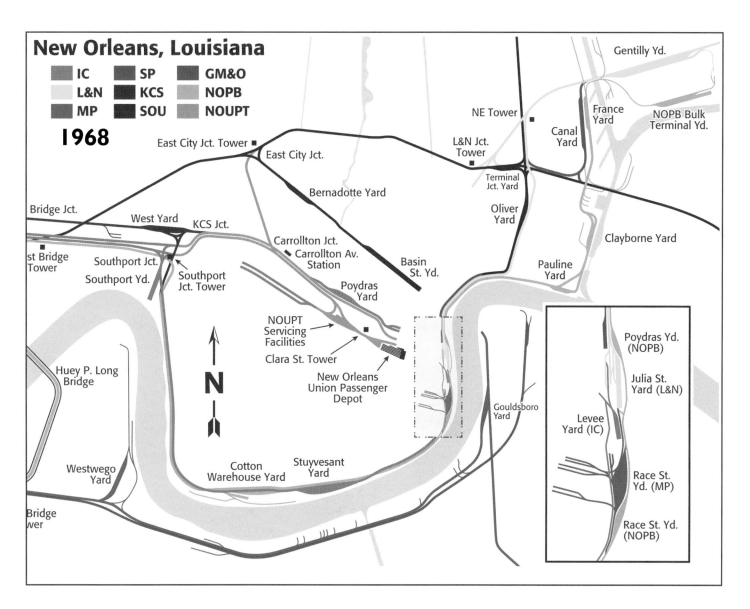

New Orleans, Louisiana

▬ IC	▬ SP	▬ GM&O
▬ L&N	▬ KCS	▬ NOPB
▬ MP	▬ SOU	▬ NOUPT

1968

East City Jct. Tower ■

East City Jct.

Bernadotte Yard

Gentilly Yd.

NE Tower

L&N Jct. Tower

France Yard

Canal Yard

NOPB Bulk Terminal Yd.

Terminal Jct. Yard

Oliver Yard

Clayborne Yard

Bridge Jct.

West Yard

KCS Jct.

Carrollton Jct.

Carrollton Av. Station

Basin St. Yd.

st Bridge Tower

Southport Jct.

Southport Yd.

Southport Jct. Tower

Poydras Yard

Pauline Yard

NOUPT Servicing Facilities

Clara St. Tower

New Orleans Union Passenger Depot

Poydras Yd. (NOPB)

Julia St. Yard (L&N)

Huey P. Long Bridge

N

Levee Yard (IC)

Gouldsboro Yard

Race St. Yd. (MP)

Westwego Yard

Cotton Warehouse Yard

Stuyvesant Yard

Race St. Yd. (NOPB)

Bridge wer

OPPOSITE: The IC and its successors maintained all the diesel switchers and roadswitchers working in New Orleans at the Mays Yard engine house. There were fourteen units at the facility on September 12, 1984, and all but three had been remanufactured at Paducah. (Jerry Sires)

RIGHT: Northbound Illinois Central train NCH (New Orleans-Markham Yard, Chicago) passes Martin Junction in Kenner, Louisiana, on October 25, 1990. The track curving to the right is a connecting track built by the ICG in 1985 that allowed southbound trains on the McComb District to turn onto the Baton Rouge District. The white KCS engines behind the IC units had been sold to a leasing company and were on their way to be rebuilt. (Jerry Sires)

BELOW: Southport Tower was built in 1912 by the Louisiana Railway & Navigation Company, a predecessor of Kansas City Southern. The old tower had served for over 80 years when photographed on May 18, 1994. It would be torn down in August 1997. (Erik Coleman)

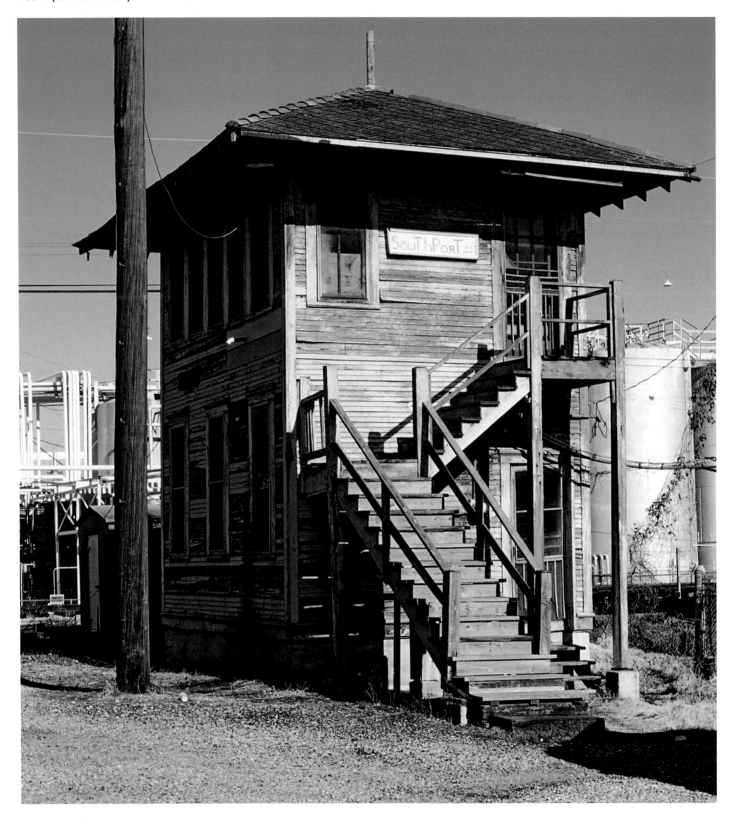

OPPOSITE ABOVE: The interlocking plant at East Bridge Junction. Tower was built by the IC in 1935 to facilitate the movement of trains on the NOPB's Huey P. Long Bridge across the Mississippi River onto and off of IC and Y&MV tracks. Remarkably, this tower remained in operation another quarter of a century after this photo of was taken on May 18, 1994. (Erik Coleman)

OPPOSITE BELOW: Illinois Central SW9 #467 was working a transfer run from IC's Stuy Docks Yard to Mays Yard on March 13, 1980. It is seen leaving the west end of the yard and is going to pass over the Nashville Avenue underpass in the foreground. (Michael M. Palmieri)

iced at Stuyvesant Yard and sent on to Levee Yard. Once the cars were loaded, they were sent back to Stuy Yard where they were weighed, assembled into 80 to 100-car trains and prepared for their fast run to points north.

Through the 1960s and 1970s, Mays Yard became the focal point of IC's operations in New Orleans. A new three-story yard office at Mays, completed in 1968, was designed to accommodate the freight office functions handled at the other IC yards in the city. The consolidation of operations at Mays Yard continued after the IC/GM&O merger of 1972. After Illinois Central handled its

last banana shipment in the early 1970s, Levee Yard was closed, and the property sold.

As ICG redefined its business model through the 1970s, the warehouses and docks at Stuyvesant Yard were sold and the intermodal terminal there was renovated. In 1984, ICG sold 20 acres of land at Stuyvesant Yard to the Board of Commissioners of the Port of New Orleans and rebuilt what remained into a small four-track yard. After Illinois Central's merger with Canadian National, the railroad relocated its intermodal facility back to Mays Yard and the remaining property at Stuyvesant Yard was sold to the Port.

BELOW: This train of Illinois coal destined for Spain arrived at New Orleans Public Belt Railroad's Cotton Warehouse Yard on November 18, 1981, behind three ICG SD20s and a GP8. The coal would be loaded aboard a ship at a bulk commodities terminal near New Orleans. The first three locomotives on the train were a class of engine built at Paducah exclusively for the ICG from 1979 to 1982. These 2000-horsepower six-motor units were built from ex-Southern Railway SD24s, ex-UP SD24s and SD24Bs, a few ex-B&O SD35s and were considered by ICG's management to be a cost-effective alternative to new locomotives at a time when the railroad's expenses were closely scrutinized by IC Industries. They soldiered on through the final years of the ICG, with none being sold to any of the new regional railroads. After Whitman Industries spun the IC off in 1988, the Moyers/Harrison management took over and developed an operating strategy that is now known as precision schedule railroading. Second-hand Burlington Northern SD40-2s were acquired and many former IC and GM&O SD40s were sent to the shop to be upgraded to meet the requirements for higher reliability. The SD20s were at the end of their careers on the IC, but many were sold to equipment dealers or short lines and continued to operate for years. (Michael M. Palmieri)

OPPOSITE ABOVE: The last car on Illinois Central train #6, the northbound "Panama Limited," has pulled away from the platform at New Orleans Union Passenger Terminal on February 13, 1971. This schedule would expire in less than three months when Amtrak took over IC's passenger operations. The Gibbons Feeds building would be torn down and the skyline in this view looking east is now dominated by the Superdome stadium. (Dennis E. Conniff, Paul Evans collection)

OPPOSITE BELOW: The "Panama" is prepared for its 4:30 p.m. departure from New Orleans on May 28, 1967. Leading today's train is #4001, one of two Illinois Central E6s that remained in service until Amtrak took over. It was one of the four purchased in 1942 for the new streamlined "Panama Limited" and, by this time, had likely accumulated more miles on the road than any IC engine without being remanufactured. (J. W. Swanberg)

OPPOSITE ABOVE: When New Orleans Union Passenger Terminal was being built in 1953, three SW8 800-horsepower switchers were ordered from EMD. Delivered in December of that year, they were used to spot head-end equipment on mail and express tracks and move equipment to the coach yard for servicing. On this April afternoon in 1961, the crew on NOUPT #2 took a break to pose for the photographer. (Charles Laird, Sr., David P. Oroszi collection)

OPPOSITE BELOW: Clara Street Tower housed this large General Railway Signal Co. interlocking machine, which controlled all NOUPT terminal trackage. Only about half of the entire machine is visible in this photo taken in April 1961. The stub-end station tracks can be seen on the right side of the photo and the throat of the station is in the center. Just out of the photo to the left are North Wye and South Wye Junctions and the connection tracks to Southport and East City Switch. Clara Street was closed on May 27, 2003, and the territory formerly controlled by the tower was transferred to Amtrak's 21st Street Tower in Chicago. With that tower's subsequent closing and demolition, control was transferred further to Amtrak's train directors in Chicago, operating from a control center on the street level of Union Station. (Charles Laird, Sr., David P. Oroszi collection)

ABOVE: All was quiet on the platforms of New Orleans Union Passenger Terminal on this April evening in 1961. In the distance, below the Gibbons Feeds building, stands NOUPT's Clara Street Tower, which controlled all traffic on the Terminal's tracks. This view is looking northwest from the terminal headhouse. (Charles Laird, Sr., David P. Oroszi collection)

Until the mid-1940s, Illinois Central's properties in Mississippi and Louisiana were divided into two parcels. One was the Memphis-New Orleans main line (with its associated branches), which ran through the center of the Magnolia State. This route was owned outright by the Illinois Central.

The other domain was the Yazoo & Mississippi Valley system, one of Illinois Central's largest subsidiaries. Known as "The Valley Route," it was comprised of a network of lines that covered much of the western half of Mississippi. The Y&MV had been chartered by a special act of the Mississippi Legislature on February 17, 1882, which gave it a unique exemption from state and local taxes for 20 years. This was intended to promote the construction of rail lines from the existing Illinois Central (Chicago, St. Louis & New Orleans) main line into the basins of the Mississippi, Yazoo and Sunflower rivers.

The Y&MV served as a second main line between Memphis and New Orleans and provided transportation for the agricultural output of the Delta region of northwestern Mississippi. This subsidiary was wholly owned by the IC and its directors were all IC officers. On July 1, 1946, it was merged into the Illinois Central.

Instead of presenting a definitive account of the Y&MV's intricate history, the scope of this chapter is a general summary of this important province of the Illinois Central. The first piece of the Yazoo & Mississippi Valley (funded by Illinois Central interests) pushed northwest from Jackson, Mississippi to Yazoo City and was completed on May 1, 1884. Over the next two years, more than 80 miles of new track was added. The Y&MV expanded dramatically in October 1892, when it absorbed the Louisville, New Orleans & Texas Railroad, giving it a main line from Memphis to New Orleans via Vicksburg and Baton Rouge.

BELOW: The operator has stepped out of the Lake Cormorant, Mississippi, depot to inspect southbound train MM-1 (Memphis-McComb, Mississippi) as it passes on October 5, 1985. L.C. Junction, where the Tallahatchie and Clarksdale Districts met, is a short distance south of the depot. (Scott D. Lindsey)

OPPOSITE ABOVE: A trio of GP40s lead a southbound train as it turns onto the Tallahatchie District at L.C. Junction on September 1973. The track in the foreground is the Clarksdale District. (David M. Johnston)

OPPOSITE BELOW: On September 29, 1990, a northbound train holds the main as southbound train CHN (Chicago Markham Yard-New Orleans) takes the siding at Crenshaw, Mississippi. (Kirk Reynolds)

Some of the early Y&MV lines were built to reach the lumber mills that went into business when harvesting of the Delta's hardwood forests began. The clearing of the land brought planters who started to produce cotton, sparking more development of the region. Several more lines and branches were built during the late 1890s and the first decade of the 20th century. By the mid-1920s, the Y&MV had grown to a 1,700-mile railroad.

During the first half of the 20th century, cotton was the Delta's primary crop and formed the traffic base for most of the Y&MV branch lines in the region. After World War II, agriculture in the Delta began to diversify. Cotton remained the dominant crop through the 1950s, but the cultivation of corn, soybeans and rice gradually took up more acreage. As the state and counties paved highways and local roads, much of the freight that was carried on the former Y&MV branches shifted from rail to trucks.

In the early 1960s, even as traffic on the Delta's branch lines was in decline, the former Yazoo & Mississippi Valley main line running south out of Memphis was still an essential IC route. The core of the Y&MV was formed by two trunk lines: the Memphis-New Orleans route and the freight route that ran from Lake Cormorant to Jackson, Mississippi.

Tallahatchie/Yazoo Districts

The northernmost segment of the Y&MV was the Tallahatchie District. It began at West Junction, where the west end of Johnston Yard tied into the Y&MV main coming from downtown Memphis. Two separate lines, the original Y&MV route (the Low Line) and the newer cut off (the High Line), met about eight miles south of West Junction at Lakeview, Mississippi.

At Lake Cormorant Junction, 7.5 miles beyond Lakeview, the two Yazoo & Mississippi Valley main lines went their separate ways. The Clarksdale District split off the Tallahatchie District and headed toward New Orleans by way of Vicksburg.

The Tallahatchie District continued 128 miles from Lake Cormorant to Gwin, where it met the Yazoo District. In the days of the steam locomotive, engines and crews were both changed at Gwin. When diesels replaced steam, crews continued to change at Gwin but engines ran through.

All of IC's Chicago/Memphis-New Orleans freight schedules were routed over the Tallahatchie and Yazoo Districts. Together, the two districts formed the Y&MV's busiest main line. Yet, this route was a single-track, "dark" railroad, bereft of automatic block

BELOW: The traveling Illinois Central freight agent paid a visit to Marks, Mississippi, on November 5, 1969, parking the Dodge van that he drove at the depot. These vans were part of a program instituted by IC to consolidate several freight agencies under one agent. (Dennis E. Conniff)

OPPOSITE ABOVE: A swinging gate protects the crossing where the Columbus & Greenville cut across the Tallahatchie District in this view looking south at Greenwood, Mississippi. Ownership of the C&G had returned to the hands of local interests about ten months before this photo on the morning of August 25, 1976. Beyond the diamond, the IC crosses Carrollton Avenue at the former IC depot. (Randy B. Olson)

OPPOSITE BELOW: On the evening of that same day, a northbound ICG freight crossed Carrollton Avenue in Greenwood. The sign that protects this crossing was a standard Illinois Central pattern that was installed at the railroad's many crossings throughout the state. (Mike McBride)

OPPOSITE ABOVE: It's late October 1997, and the cotton is ready to be harvested as southbound train CRGE (Conrail Effingham, Illinois-Geismar, Louisiana) passes through Rising Sun, Mississippi. (Kirk Reynolds)

OPPOSITE BELOW: Northbound train FEME crosses a trestle near the Morgan Brake National Wildlife Refuge north of Tchula, Mississippi, on June 27, 1997. This schedule originated at Ferguson, Mississippi, located east of Brookhaven on the former Mississippi Central Railroad, and ran to Johnston Yard in Memphis. (Bill E. Dressler)

ABOVE: A pair of SD70s hustle a southbound Cargill grain train down the Yazoo District on October 21, 1997. The train is passing the Westfield Plantation, a couple of miles south of Tchula, Mississippi. While the farm's sign features a cotton boll, agriculture in the Delta has diversified so corn and soybeans are also important crops in the region. (Kirk Reynolds)

signals. Train movements were governed by timetable and train order. The railroad's hottest dispatch freights ducked in and out of sidings that were spaced 10 or 20 miles apart. It's easy to see why IC provided its swift passenger trains an exclusive racetrack largely devoid of freight traffic to speed them through northern Mississippi.

By the mid-1980s, beyond the main lines, only a few secondary lines and branches of the once-extensive Y&MV empire survived. One such branch was the Sunflower District, which was composed of three lines. The first line ran in a northwest direction from the junction with the Tallahatchie District at Swan Lake to Clarksdale, where it joined the Memphis-New Orleans "Valley Route." The second leg of the Sunflower District ran southward almost 88 miles from Tutwiler (between Swan Lake and Clarksdale) to Yazoo Junction, where it connected to the Yazoo District. The third piece of the Sunflower District ran north from Tutwiler for a little more than six miles to Vance. Illinois Central Gulf abandoned the Sunflower District from Yazoo Junction to Belzoni in 1977 and from Belzoni to Vance in 1981.

Another secondary line, the Tchula District, ran eastward from the Yazoo District at Gwin for about 25 miles to the Water

Valley District at Durant. This branch was abandoned in sections from 1978 to 1982.

The Yazoo District was 70 miles long. The first half of the district south of Gwin was flat, running across the Delta country. But, a few miles south of Yazoo City (at Valley), the rails turned southeast and started up Anding Grade, an eight-mile ascent into the hills that overlook the floodplain. Beyond the crest of the grade at Anding, the Yazoo District encountered a couple more (but less severe) grades before arriving at North Jackson.

The Valley Route

The former main line of the Louisville, New Orleans & Texas was the backbone of the Y&MV. The 435-mile route (between Lake Cormorant and New Orleans) was divided into four districts. The Clarksdale, Cleveland and Vicksburg Districts ran through rural western Mississippi while the Baton Rouge District was primarily an industrial switching operation that ran between its namesake city and New Orleans.

Through passenger service between Memphis and New Orleans over the Y&MV lasted until 1950 when the "Planter" was

OPPOSITE ABOVE: This scene, chronicled at Bentonia, Mississippi, on August 31, 1986, contains all the elements that typified the Illinois Central Gulf in the Magnolia State: Paducah Geeps, flatcars loaded with lumber products and the deserted Y&MV depot. This is northbound train NM-4, a New Orleans-Memphis schedule. (Scott D. Lindsey)

OPPOSITE BELOW: The Yazoo and Canton Districts converged at the north end of North Jackson Yard. This view, taken from the Woodrow Wilson Avenue overpass, shows southbound CN-5 coming off the Yazoo District on September 1, 1986. In the distance, the old roundhouse stands between the two main lines. (Scott D. Lindsey)

ABOVE: For many years, a road switcher was assigned to work the local industries around Tunica, Mississippi, and to serve customers on the Helena District. In 1974, the Tunica road switcher job was abolished and the switching duties at Tunica and the remaining portion of the Helena District were taken over by local freights #191/192. By the time this photo was taken on May 16, 1975, the Clarksdale switcher was coming north to Tunica three times a week to work Tunica and the Helena District. The engine and caboose for this job are parked in the house track at the Tunica depot in this view looking north on the Clarksdale District. (Dennis E. Conniff)

discontinued. The final chapter of Illinois Central passenger service on the former Y&MV lines was closed when the "Delta Express" made its last run between Memphis and Greenville, Mississippi, on March 27, 1965.

The Clarksdale District ran 93 miles from Lake Cormorant to Cleveland. Two branch lines still connected with the Clarksdale District in the early 1960s. The first was the Helena District, which ran northward from Jonestown (a few miles east of the main line) and then turned toward Lula, where it crossed the Clarksdale District. It continued westward about eight miles to Trotter's Point on the Mississippi River.

The Helena District was unique on two counts. It held the distinction of including the only track that the Illinois Central operated in Arkansas and that track was reached by the last car ferry that the IC operated, the "Pelican." Car ferry service between Trotter's Point and Helena, Arkansas, dated back to 1889 and the "Pelican" was the last of a series of steam-powered car ferries that carried cars and locomotives across the Mississippi River. In the early

1960s, the superstructure and engines of the "Pelican" were removed and it became an unpowered barge. The towboat "William B. Barnett" was assigned to power the barge. In 1973, the Interstate Commerce Commission granted the Illinois Central permission to abandon the Helena District between Lula and Trotter's Point as well as its property in Arkansas. The rest of the district between Lula and Jonestown remained in operation.

The second branch split off from the Clarksdale District at the city of Clarksdale. This was the Sunflower District, which ran down to Swan Lake to meet the Tallahatchie District.

The Clarksdale District joined the Cleveland District at Cleveland, Mississippi. Trains working out of Memphis and Vicksburg changed crews at this terminal. The Cleveland District spanned about 107 miles and in 1960 there was a single branch that diverged from it.

The Leland District extended northwest from the main line at Leland for about 7.5 miles to Metcalf, where it connected with the Riverside District. The Riverside District had once been a 127-

OPPOSITE: It's the first day of April 1972 and a pair of Illinois Central GP9s pull a mixed train of IC boxcars and covered hoppers northward at Tunica, Mississippi. The merger with the GM&O is four months away and the Clarksdale District is still an important main line, which is evident from the replaced ties laying trackside. (Two photos, David M. Johnston)

BELOW: The "Pelican" was a steam-powered transfer boat operated by the Illinois Central between Trotter's Point, Mississippi, and Helena, Arkansas. It was the last of the railroad's maritime operations. The "Pelican" and its sister "Albatross" both served as the link between IC's Meridian and Vicksburg Districts at Vicksburg until the Vicksburg Bridge & Terminal Company opened the rail and highway bridge across the Mississippi River in 1930. The "Albatross" was sold and the "Pelican" was sent to Trotter's point to replace a smaller boat. In the mid-1950s, plans were drawn up to convert the "Pelican" to diesel power, but were never implemented. The boilers, machinery and superstructure and the hull was renamed ICRR Barge B-109. To move the barge between the ramps, the Illinois Central bought towboat "William B. Barnett." The two vessels are seen at Helena, Arkansas, in April 1968. The ferry service between Trotter's Point and Helena ceased operation in 1972, ending the IC's long history of car ferry operations. (Morgan McIlwain)

mile secondary route that paralleled the main line from Coahoma (where it met the Clarksdale District) to Riverside Junction (where it met the Cleveland District). By 1960, the northern and southern portions of the line had been abandoned, leaving the middle 32 miles of the district intact. This segment allowed the Illinois Central to reach Greenville, the largest city in the Delta.

The Cleveland District crossed the Columbus & Greenville Railroad at Elizabeth, a couple of miles north of Leland. In 1985, ten years after C&G regained its independence from Illinois Central Gulf, the short line expanded by purchasing part of the Cleveland District and other ex-Y&MV trackage around Greenville from ICG.

The Redwood District was the last new section of railroad to be built by the Illinois Central. It connected with the Yazoo District at Valley and ran 29 miles to Redwood Junction on the Cleveland District north of Vicksburg. Completed in late 1967, the line was constructed to carry pulpwood and chemicals to a large new paper mill five miles from its southern end.

However, the northern end of the line served only eight years before most of it (20 miles) was shut down in 1975. Nine miles of track at the district's southern end remained in place to serve the paper mill. In several places the line had been built close to the Yazoo River and the ground in these areas proved to be very unstable. The roadbed and track had a continual tendency to "creep"

toward the river, making track maintenance an on-going struggle. This resulted in the early abandonment of the line between Redwood Yard (a mile north of the mill) and Valley. Six miles of track at the district's southern end remained in place to serve the paper mill. This trackage, along with 20 miles of former main line running north and south of Vicksburg, were included in the sale to MidSouth Rail in 1986.

Vicksburg, the largest city on the Mississippi River between Memphis and Baton Rouge, was the southern end of the Cleveland District. It was also the junction where IC's Meridian, Mississippi-Shreveport, Louisiana, main line met the Valley Route. Both routes converged at Freight Yard. Freight schedules that operated over both routes were coordinated to exchange blocks of cars at Vicksburg.

The first railroad to serve Vicksburg was the Clinton & Vicksburg, one of the lines that would eventually become part of IC's Meridian District. The C&V's station facilities were built at the top of the bluff overlooking the river. When the New Orleans, Baton Rouge, Vicksburg & Memphis Railroad (a predecessor of IC's Valley Route) was building through Vicksburg in 1882, its engineers followed a course below the bluffs. For the two railroads to interchange traffic, the older line (which was by then named the Vicksburg & Meridian Railroad) built a connection southward to the new railroad.

The longest segment of the Valley Route was the Vicksburg District, running 142 miles from Vicksburg to North Baton Rouge. In the early 1960s, the district crossed a secondary Illinois Central route and a shortline railroad. There were also two IC branch lines that diverged from the Vicksburg District.

Reaching 98 miles from Jackson, Mississippi, to Natchez on the Mississippi River, Illinois Central's Natchez District intersected only one other rail line, the Vicksburg District at Harriston, Mississippi. There was a small yard at this junction where trains on the Vicksburg District would pick up and set out cars for the Natchez District.

At Roxie, Mississippi, the Vicksburg District crossed the short line Mississippi Central Railroad. Acquired by Illinois Central in 1967, the Mississippi Central became IC's Central District. When much of the Natchez District was abandoned in 1979, the Central District became ICG's sole route to Natchez.

Two branches jutted from the Vicksburg District: the Clinton District and the Woodville District. The Clinton District was the smaller of the two, extending eastward from the main line at Ethel, Louisiana, to its namesake town, Clinton. The 8.3-mile branch was

an early casualty of ICG's agenda to discard underperforming trackage and was abandoned on December 22, 1977.

The Vicksburg District's other branch, the 41.6-mile Woodville District, was an L-shaped appendage that ran westward from the main line at Slaughter, Louisiana. The upper end of the district between Argue, Louisiana, and Woodville, Mississippi, held the distinction of being the earliest piece of railroad built that eventually became part of the Illinois Central. This railroad was built as the West Feliciana Railroad to connect Woodville with the riverboat landing at Bayou Sara. It became part of the Louisville, New Orleans & Texas in 1888 and, then part of the IC subsidiary Y&MV in 1892.

The northern end of the Woodville District between Woodville and Harwood was abandoned by ICG on October 29, 1978. Most of the remaining trackage of the district remained intact when the Illinois Central regained its identity in 1989 and it eventually became part of the Canadian National system.

Approaching Louisiana's capitol city, the Valley Route transitioned from a country railroad into a line running through the middle of a 90-mile industrial corridor. Just north of Baton Rouge

BELOW: The depot at Leland, Mississippi, was located in the middle of the wye that connected the Leland District with the main line Cleveland District. During the era when Illinois Central operated passenger trains on the Y&MV main line, they used this wye to reach Greenville. In this view looking northward taken on February 13, 1982, the Leland Switcher is parked on the south leg of the wye. (David M. Johnston)

OPPOSITE ABOVE: As Illinois Central converted from steam locomotives to diesels, some auxiliary water tenders (cisterns in IC parlance) were converted to haul diesel fuel and sand to remote engine terminals around the system. One of these fuel and sand cars, the X559, was stationed at the small engine facility at Greenville, Mississippi, on August 25, 1976. (Mike McBride)

OPPOSITE BELOW: In the early 20th century, Tutwiler, Mississippi, was the junction of two prominent Y&MV lines. But by the time this photo was taken in February 1970, it had declined to the status of the station where the Sunflower District's two branches extended from its Clarksdale-Swan Lake trunk. (Dennis E. Conniff)

ABOVE: On its way to switch local industries, Illinois Central Gulf SW9 #462 crosses over the eastbound lanes of U.S. Highway 190 and under the east railroad approach to the Huey P. Long Bridge at Baton Rouge, Louisiana, on October 9, 1980. Not to be confused with the highway/railroad bridge near New Orleans which was also named after Governor Long, this bridge carried Kansas City Southern and Missouri Pacific trains across the Mississippi River. (Michael M. Palmieri)

Yard, the Vicksburg District passed under the east approach of the Mississippi River rail-highway bridge. Opened in 1940, this structure carried trains of the Missouri Pacific and Kansas City Southern, as well as U.S. Highway 190. About a half of a mile south of the bridge, the Vicksburg and Baton Rouge Districts met at MP Junction. This junction was at the north end of IC's North Baton Rouge Yard. Passenger trains on the Missouri Pacific's subsidiary New Orleans, Texas & Mexico, one of a group of railroads identified as the Gulf Coast Lines, exercised trackage rights over the Baton Rouge District between MP Junction and New Orleans. This arrangement began with a subsidiary of the Frisco in 1910 and lasted until 1967 when the last MP passenger trains into New Orleans were discontinued. Missouri Pacific's GCL freight traffic was also handled by IC into and out of the Crescent City.

The Baton Rouge District was 101 miles long and had become one of Illinois Central's most lucrative properties. While the IC encountered the Mississippi River and its tributaries in many communities, the river below Baton Rouge is different in that it is deep enough for ocean-going vessels. A combination of an unlimited supply of fresh water needed for many industrial operations, a convenient source of petroleum, and barge access to the Mississippi River and Gulf Intracoastal Waterway systems made the land along the Baton Rouge District a very attractive location for oil refineries and chemical plants. This development began when Standard Oil opened one of the country's largest oil refineries at Baton Rouge in 1905. It gradually grew over the next 35 years and then took off when America's entry into the Second World War created an unprecedented demand for fuel, octane enhancing fuel additives and synthetic rubber.

In the post-war years, these industries provided a steady flow of high-value traffic to the IC. The railroad also brought grain to elevators and coal to docks that loaded those commodities onto ships. Most of the chemical traffic was marshalled through the district's main classification facilities, North Baton Rouge Yard and Geismar Yard. There were smaller yards located near higher concentrations of industrial plants along the district at Lutcher,

OPPOSITE ABOVE: At North Baton Rouge Yard, GP10 #8023 and an ex-GM&O unit rested next to the turntable while GP9 #9325, GP10 #8071 and GP40 #3061 were parked at the fuel rack on May 17, 1979. In addition to servicing the engines assigned to all the yard jobs and locals operating on the Baton Rouge District, this facility also attended to power for trains running north to Vicksburg and Memphis. (Michael M. Palmieri)

OPPOSITE BELOW: The southbound Second Geismar Turn rolls past the former Y&MV Baton Rouge passenger station on October 9, 1980. After passenger service through Baton Rouge ended in 1958, the building was sold to the City of Baton Rouge and now serves as home to the Louisiana Arts and Science Center. Immediately beyond the train is the levee that protects Baton Rouge from the Mississippi River which looms in the background. (Michael M. Palmieri)

ABOVE: Illinois Central Gulf GP10 #8077 was parked on the siding in front of the Good Hope yard office on March 18, 1983, amidst the surrounding industrial complex. (Jerry Sires)

Reserve, Good Hope and Destrehan. Trains out of North Baton Rouge, Geismar and New Orleans shuttled traffic between these terminals, where dispatch freights would forward their cargo to IC terminals at Memphis, St. Louis and Chicago.

The Hammond District served as a critical link between the Valley Route and the McComb District, part of the Memphis-New Orleans main line. This line reached eastward from North Baton Rouge Yard to Hammond, Louisiana, a distance of about 44 miles.

The Meridian-Shreveport Route

Most of the Illinois Central's main lines were oriented along a north-south axis, but there were two notable exceptions. One was IC's Iowa Division, running west from Chicago and across northern Illinois and Iowa. The other significant departure from the north-south principle was Illinois Central's secondary main line between Meridian, Mississippi, and Shreveport, Louisiana. The uncommon alignment of this route is due to fact that it was one of the IC's last major acquisitions.

The origins of this route can be traced back to 1831 when Vicksburg was but a small port on the Mississippi River. Local interests chartered the Clinton & Vicksburg Railroad to build a line eastward from Vicksburg. Even before construction of the line began in 1833, its promoters were considering building all the way to Jackson. The railroad was completed as far as Clinton in 1838 and, two years later, it became the first railroad to reach Jackson.

In the meantime, another railroad was founded in 1836 to build a line east of Jackson. Construction of the 14-mile Jackson & Brandon Railroad & Bridge Company was finished between its namesake towns in February 1850.

In 1846, the Southern Railroad of Mississippi (which was not associated with the Southern Railway that was incorporated in 1894) was organized to connect Brandon with the Mississippi & Alabama Railroad at the Mississippi-Alabama state line. No track was laid before the charter lapsed in 1850, but another charter was granted later that year. At first, progress was slow. The Southern acquired the J&BR&BC in 1852 and work began on the line east of Brandon. By 1858, 21 miles of railroad had been built to Morton, Mississippi.

As work on the Southern Railroad proceeded eastward from Morton, another construction crew was building the Mobile & Ohio Railroad northward through eastern Mississippi. The M&O

established a station at a town called Sowashee in 1855. Five years later, the town was renamed Meridian. The Southern Railroad of Mississippi completed its line to Meridian in June 1861.

Construction of the western half of IC's Meridian-Shreveport route was started much later than that of the eastern half. The Vicksburg, Shreveport & Texas Railroad was incorporated in March 1852 as part of a grand scheme to build a railroad across Louisiana and Texas that would eventually reach the Pacific Ocean at San Diego. Another road, the Texas Western Railroad had been chartered in Texas to construct the portion of the Pacific Railroad that would cross the Lone Star State.

By the time the southern states began to secede from the Union in the spring of 1861, 72 miles of railroad had been built between Delta Point (across the river from Vicksburg) and Monroe, Louisiana. Another section of the VS&T was also in operation between Shreveport and Marshall, Texas. While the railroad across Mississippi was built to the common southern gauge of 60 inches, the VS&T was 66 inches, which was being used in Texas, Arkansas and Missouri.

The Civil War brought about the destruction of much of the VS&T, as well as the Southern Railroad of Mississippi. As both lines slowly recovered from the war, they underwent changes in their identities. The Southern Railroad of Mississippi became the

Vicksburg & Meridian while the VS&T was reorganized as the North Louisiana & Texas Railroad and then as the Vicksburg, Shreveport & Pacific Railroad.

In 1881, the VS&P came under the control of British interests led by merchant banker Baron Emile Beauford d'Erlanger. This group owned a group of southern railroads that were collectively known as the Queen and Crescent Route. The deep pockets of the VS&P's new owners made it possible to finally complete the route between Vicksburg and Shreveport in 1884. The Queen & Crescent Route's owners had also obtained the majority of Vicksburg & Meridian stock and took control of that road on February 1, 1889. The V&M was soon renamed Alabama & Vicksburg Railway. With both lines under common ownership, the VS&P and A&V were designated the Vicksburg Route. For the next 35 years, the Vicksburg Route prospered and both lines were rebuilt to high standards.

Baron Erlanger held control of the two roads until 1924 when he sold his shares of VS&P and A&V stock on the New York and New Orleans markets. Illinois Central's subsidiary Yazoo & Mississippi Valley leased both roads for 365 years in 1926. The A&V became the Meridian District and the VS&P became the Shreveport District. While the independent Vicksburg Route had served as a bridge route between the southeast and southwest, as

BELOW: The large petroleum refinery at Good Hope, Louisiana, provided a substantial amount of high-revenue traffic for the IC/ICG. On December 15, 1983, GP10 #8116 was switching a cut of tank cars that carried the chemical byproducts of the refining process. (Michael M. Palmieri)

OPPOSITE ABOVE: On May 12, 1979, a crewman on ICG #8000 steps outside to take in the sights and sounds of Amtrak train #20, the northbound "Crescent," as it accelerates from the Meridian depot. (Michael M. Palmieri)

OPPOSITE BELOW: The combination depot/freight house at Forest, Mississippi, was a scheduled stop for IC's Meridian-Shreveport passenger trains until that service ended on this route in 1967. A couple of years after the passenger trains were gone, the station was still handling freight business with a Bangor & Aroostook refrigerator car and an Erie-Lackawanna boxcar parked at the loading dock on October 17, 1969. (Dennis E. Conniff)

part of the Illinois Central, the role of the Meridian-Shreveport route was to act as a feeder to IC's north-south main lines.

In 1882, after both railroads had been converted to standard gauge, a train ferry began operating across the Mississippi River between Vicksburg and the eastern end of the Vicksburg, Shreveport & Pacific at Delta Point, Louisiana. Ferry service began with a used vessel, "Northern Pacific No. 1," which had been built for the NP in 1879. The subsequent ferries were all built new: "Delta" in 1891, "Pelican" in 1902 and "Albatross" in 1907. Ferry service continued under IC ownership as the Louisiana & Mississippi Railroad Transfer Co. until the opening of a rail-highway bridge in 1930.

The two lines that had formed the Vicksburg Route were physically connected on April 28, 1930, when the bridge across the Mississippi River was opened to traffic. Built by Vicksburg Bridge & Terminal Company, the bridge was designed to carry a two-lane roadway for vehicular traffic and a single-track railroad. The Y&MV leased the railroad portion of the bridge. After the bridge opened, the "Pelican" was transferred to the IC's Trotter's Point, Mississippi-Helena, Arkansas, crossing.

Most of the interchange traffic on the Meridian District was handled through Meridian, where IC connected with Southern Railway, Gulf, Mobile & Ohio and the short line Meridian & Bigbee. Illinois Central also maintained an interchange at Newton (about 31 miles west of Meridian) where GM&O's line crossed. The passenger trains of the three trunkline railroads shared Meridian's Union Depot.

The Shreveport District had far more junctions with other railroads than the Meridian District. Missouri Pacific interchanged with the Shreveport District at four locations: Tallulah, Delhi, Rayville, and Monroe (where IC also connected with Arkansas & Louisiana Missouri). The Rock Island's Little Rock, Arkansas-Eunice, Louisiana, "Little Rock" line crossed the Shreveport District at Ruston. At Gibsland, the IC connected with two short lines: the Louisiana & North West, which entered from the north, and the North Louisiana & Gulf, which came in from the south. At Sibley, the IC crossed the main line of Kansas City Southern subsidiary Louisiana & Arkansas.

Shreveport, Louisiana, was the busiest interchange point on the Shreveport District. The city was the operating hub of Kansas

BELOW: Steam power of a fashion was still alive on the IC on January 12, 1967, in the form of derrick X89. It is seen here next to the Pelahatchie, Mississippi, depot either preparing to go to work or finishing a job. (Dennis E. Conniff)

OPPOSITE ABOVE: Westbound dispatch freight MS-9, train #269, waits in the siding at Crew Lake, Louisiana, in November 1975 for its scheduled meet with local freight #298 and dispatch freight SM-2, train #262. Illinois Central Gulf GP9 #9380 is leading three other Geeps. (James B. Holder, Steve H. Forrest collection)

OPPOSITE BELOW: East Monroe Tower protected the diamond where the Shreveport District crossed the Missouri Pacific in Monroe, Louisiana. On June 4, 1985, a GP8 was working the Illinois Central Gulf yard at East Monroe. This view is looking east. (Michael M. Palmieri)

OPPOSITE ABOVE: Illinois Central had a small roundhouse near its passenger depot at Monroe. The turntable remained in service for years after the roundhouse was torn down. Illinois Central Gulf GP35 #2522 is parked on the turntable lead on June 4, 1985. (Michael M. Palmieri)

OPPOSITE BELOW: The last IC passenger trains stopped at the Monroe depot on March 30, 1968. Aside from the absence of passengers, it still looked like a working passenger station on February 20, 1977. (Michael M. Palmieri)

ABOVE: Passing over the vegetation on ICG's Shreveport District, this eastbound train is about to cross North Fourth Street in Monroe, Louisiana, in August 1973. (Tom Sink)

City Southern and its subsidiary, Louisiana & Arkansas. Two subsidiaries of Southern Pacific, the Cotton Belt and Texas & New Orleans, also served Shreveport. And Texas & Pacific Railway (controlled by Missouri Pacific) entered Shreveport from three different directions.

Illinois Central purchased the Tremont & Gulf Railway on August 1, 1959. The line branched off the Shreveport District at West Monroe and ran south almost 61 miles to Winnfield, Louisiana. Practically all of the district was abandoned in March

1986, save for about four miles of track at Winnfield that was sold to Kansas City Southern.

The Meridian and Shreveport Districts were among the first parts of the IC to be fully dieselized. The route's last passenger train – the eastbound "Northeastern Limited" and westbound "Southwestern Limited" – was pulled by one or two boiler-equipped GP7s. These trains were discontinued on the Meridian District on October 24, 1967, and on the Shreveport District on March 30, 1968.

OPPOSITE ABOVE: Illinois Central Gulf GP8 #7986 pauses at the Arcadia, Louisiana, depot on February 8, 1977. The building has been preserved and is now a local history museum. (Michael M. Palmieri)

OPPOSITE BELOW: There's a lot going on in this view looking east from the Sparta Street overpass in Gibsland on August 19, 1977. In the center of the photo, the rear-end crew is out on the platform of their caboose at the end of a long eastbound train. Near the diamond, an IC Geep sits on the L&NW with a caboose and a couple of cars. On the interchange track, three L&NW engines with a string of cars wait for their turn to go to work. (Jay J Ruediger, Cliff Scholes collection)

ABOVE: A westbound ICG freight led by low-nosed GP18 #9424 bangs across the L&NW diamond at Gibsland, Louisiana, on April 20, 1978. The engine would be sold to Columbia & Silver Creek Railroad in December 1983. (David E. Lichtenberg)

Demise of the Y&MV

In the wake of the IC/GM&O merger, operating patterns on the new railroad began to change. The Valley Route came to be regarded as a redundant main line by IC Industries' directors. Some of the traffic that had been handled over the former Y&MV main line through Vicksburg was redirected out of Baton Rouge to Hammond and then northward to Jackson, Mississippi, and on to Memphis, though some traffic continued to move north from Baton Rouge.

The Homochitto River crossing and its approaches at Rosetta, Mississippi, 63 miles north of Baton Rouge, had been a recurring source of maintenance and repair for the railroad. Major floods in March 1955 and April 1974 had washed the bridge out. Both times it was repaired, but the first section of the New Orleans-Memphis line to be abandoned (54 miles between Crosby and Port Gibson in 1981) was the one on which the troublesome Homochitto crossing was located.

With the Valley Route no longer connecting Memphis and New Orleans, all the northbound traffic from the Baton Rouge area had to move over the Hammond District to the McComb District. Traffic from the Geismar area eventually began moving south to the New Orleans area and then north on the McComb District. Through traffic between Vicksburg and Memphis continued to traverse the Cleveland and Clarksdale districts, but time was running out for that piece of the old Y&MV, too. Several long segments of the line were abandoned from early 1983 through the summer of 1985.

The remaining section of the Sunflower District from Swan Lake to Clarksdale was sold to Gulf & Ohio Railways on December 31, 1985. The purchase also included a section of the Clarksdale District, which ran north from Clarksdale to Lula and the Helena District from Lula to Jonestown. The new short line was named the Mississippi Delta Railroad.

The Columbus & Greenville Railway acquired three former Y&MV lines from ICG in May 1985. The purchase included the Cleveland District from Cleveland to Hollandale and the Leland and Riverside Districts from Leland into Greenville (which, by then, were both part of the Cleveland District). The Riverside District north of Metcalf to Rosedale had been sold to the Rosedale-Bolivar County Port Commission in 1979 and was operated as the Great River Railroad.

The largest parcel of the old Y&MV to be sold by ICG was the Meridian, Mississippi-Shreveport, Louisiana, route. In addition to the east-west line, the transaction also included nine miles of the Vicksburg District running south from Vicksburg to LeTourneau, the remaining 11 miles of the Cleveland District north of Vicksburg to Redwood Junction and the remaining six miles of the Redwood District from Redwood Jct. to Redwood Yard. Rounding out the deal was 70 miles of the former Gulf & Ship Island between Hattiesburg and Gulfport, Mississippi, and a short section of the Winnfield District at West Monroe, Louisiana.

When the Illinois Central Railroad was spun off by Whitman Industries in 1989, only three significant pieces of former Yazoo & Mississippi Valley trackage were part of it: the Memphis-Jackson freight line, the Baton Rouge District and the Hammond District. The Tallahatchie District was combined into the Yazoo District in 1993. In an odd twist of fate, Amtrak decided to reroute the famed "City of New Orleans" train over the former Y&MV between Memphis, Tennessee, and Jackson, Mississippi, in 1995, bringing Chicago-New Orleans passenger service to a route that never had it before.

BELOW: An eastbound Illinois Central Gulf freight is about to cross the Louisiana & North West Railroad at Gibsland, Louisiana, on March 26, 1975. The gate provided protection for train movements through this crossing. Its normal position was lined against the L&NW. (James P. Marcus, Joe McMillan collection)

OPPOSITE ABOVE: Illinois Central Gulf's yard at Shreveport, Louisiana, was actually across the Red River in Bossier City. Pairs of Paducah Geeps, GP30s and GP38s were tied up at the Bossier City engine facility on May 23, 1985. (Michael M. Palmieri)

OPPOSITE BELOW: Eastbound Illinois Central passenger train #208, the Shreveport-Meridian "Northeastern Limited," stands ready for its 5:00 pm departure at Shreveport Union Station on December 30, 1964. The train will first back out of the station and then head eastward on the Shreveport District. (Louis A. Marre)

TOP: In the late 1940s, the Illinois Central installed this billboard near the former site of Poplar Avenue Station in Memphis. Facing North Front Street and the city's business district, it assured Memphians they could always count on the IC no matter the weather conditions. At the time, the railroad was investing heavily in new passenger trains while facing increasing competition from airlines and automobiles. The sign was still in place and in reasonably good shape in the 1970s when this photo was taken, but it was no longer relevant. The IC had become the ICG and rail passenger service to Memphis was handled by Amtrak. At the beginning of the third decade of the 21st century, Memphis is, more than ever, an important regional transportation center for rail, highway, air and maritime transport and IC successor Canadian National carries on the promise of this sign, moving traffic into, out of and through the city, weather notwithstanding. (David M. Johnston)

ABOVE: Freshly-painted ICG #199375 is carrying the markers on this Illinois Central Gulf freight train at Paducah, Kentucky, in June 1976. This car was part of the last group of cabooses delivered to the Illinois Central which were built at the Centralia, Illinois, car shops in 1971. (Randy B. Olson)

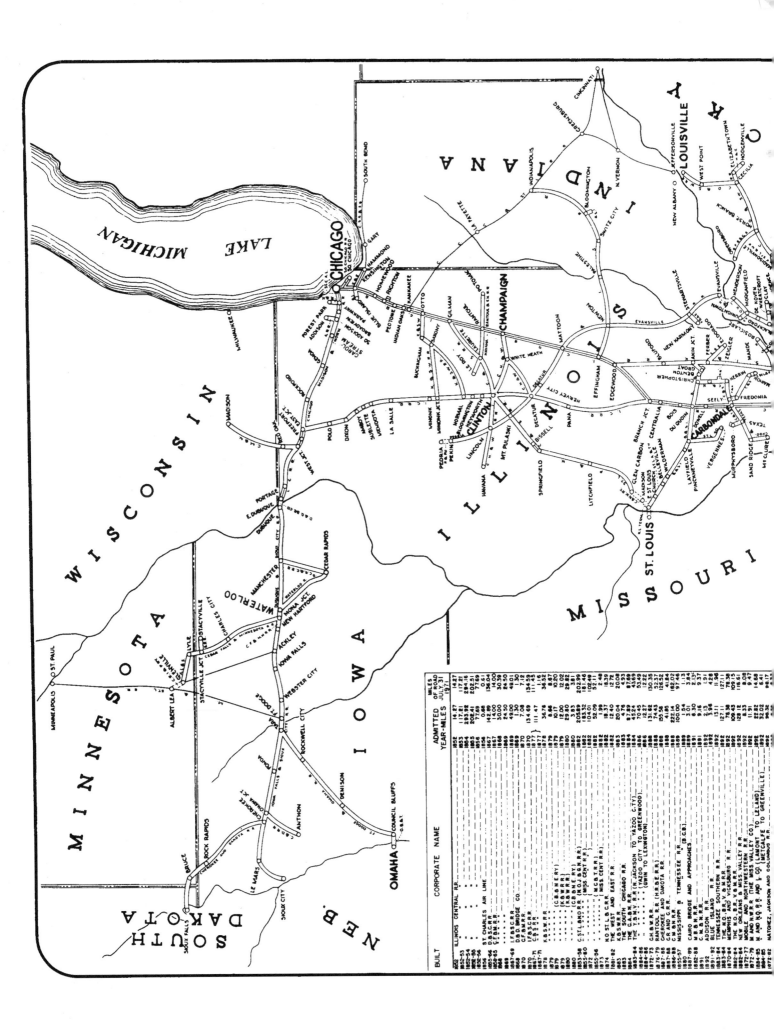